The Dancer and the Dance

The Dancer and the Dance

Essays on Skepticism and the Search for Meaning

MICHAEL WASSERMAN

WIPF & STOCK · Eugene, Oregon

THE DANCER AND THE DANCE
Essays on Skepticism and the Search for Meaning

Copyright © 2022 Michael Wasserman. All rights reserved. Except for brief quotations in critical publications or reviews, no part of this book may be reproduced in any manner without prior written permission from the publisher. Write: Permissions, Wipf and Stock Publishers, 199 W. 8th Ave., Suite 3, Eugene, OR 97401.

Wipf & Stock
An Imprint of Wipf and Stock Publishers
199 W. 8th Ave., Suite 3
Eugene, OR 97401

www.wipfandstock.com

PAPERBACK ISBN: 978-1-6667-3601-4
HARDCOVER ISBN: 978-1-6667-9378-9
EBOOK ISBN: 978-1-6667-9379-6

JUNE 7, 2022 10:32 AM

An earlier version of "Overlapping Magisteria" appeared in *Zeramim: An Online Journal of Applied Jewish Thought* 3:1 (Fall 2018) 69–80.

An earlier version of "Consciousness of Consciousness" appeared in *Modeh Ani: The Transcendent Prayer of Gratitude*, edited by David Birnbaum and Martin S. Cohen, 153–61. New York: New Paradigm Matrix, 2017.

An earlier version of "The Dancer and the Dance" appeared in *Conservative Judaism* 53:3 (Spring 2001) 3–16.

An earlier version of "The New Middle Ground" appeared in *Conservative Judaism* 63:3 (Spring 2012) 3–13.

An earlier version of "The Divine 'I Will Be'" appeared under the title "The Ehyeh of Presence" in *Ehyeh Asher Ehyeh*, edited by David Birnbaum and Martin S. Cohen, 23–31. New York: New Paradigm Matrix, 2019.

Contents

Acknowledgments | ix

List of Abbreviations | x

Introduction | xi

OVERLAPPING MAGISTERIA | 1

DOVER BEACH | 14

CONSCIOUSNESS OF CONSCIOUSNESS | 23

THE EXILE OF LANGUAGE | 33

THE DANCER AND THE DANCE | 41

THE NEW MIDDLE GROUND | 62

THE DIVINE "I-WILL-BE" | 74

THE VIA NEGATIVA | 85

Bibliography | 97

Acknowledgments

I am grateful to those who helped to bring this short book to completion. My teacher Arthur Green gave generously of his time over the years to read drafts of several of these essays and to offer valuable criticism and advice. Another of my teachers, the late David Hartman, read the original version of the title essay many years ago and graciously encouraged me. My colleague Martin Cohen edited earlier versions of several of these essays for the journal *Conservative Judaism* and the Mesora Matrix anthologies. I am fortunate to have received his wisdom and support. My friend Leora Zeitlin helped to prepare this collection for publication and offered helpful insights and advice along the way. My children, Hannah, Gabriel, and Jonathan, encouraged me as well and kept after me to finish this project when I was slow to do so. Most of all, I am grateful to my wife, Elana Kanter, without whose love and support I would never have written these essays at all (in addition to being my soul mate, Elana is my co-rabbi at the synagogue that we founded together almost two decades ago). At every step in the process, she was a constant source of encouragement, as well as a skilled and sensitive critic. I dedicate this book to her, with love and admiration.

List of Abbreviations

BT Eruvin	Babylonian Talmud Tractate Eruvin
JT Pe'ah	Jerusalem Talmud Tractate Pe'ah
Pesikta DRK	Pesikta d'Rav Kahanna
M Avot	Mishnah Tractate Avot
MT Teshuvah	Mishneh Torah Hilkhot Teshuvah
Num. Rabbah	Numbers Rabbah
BT Ber.	Babylonian Talmud Tractate Berakhot
Mekh. Baholdesh	Mekhilta of Rabbi Ishmael Tractate Bahodesh
Gen. Rabbah	Genesis Rabbah

Introduction

Can a seeker also be a skeptic? Can one believe without renouncing the responsibility to doubt?

Those who will not choose between their heart and head, who yearn for truths that they can live by but refuse to purchase those truths at the price of intellectual integrity, struggle with what seems to be an unresolvable dilemma. Their need for meaning and their fear of self-deception pull them in opposite directions. At one level, the problem is that critical thinking clashes with particular religious claims. Geological research undermines Genesis. Archaeology is at odds with Exodus.

But the problem is deeper than that, and hence, broader as well. Faith and skepticism are in tension not only in that they make incompatible claims but in that they inhabit incompatible vantage points. They differ not only in what they teach but in where they teach from.

To be a skeptic is to view the world from a position of detachment rather than dependence, of aloneness rather than allegiance. It is to step back to such a psychological distance that loyalty to anything except cold evidence seems dishonest, a surrender of integrity. The core imperative of the skeptic is to think for oneself, to deny authority to anything beyond the independent intellect.

Meaning, on the other hand, is a matter of engagement. To embrace a faith is to stand *for*, to live by principles. But more

Introduction

fundamentally, it is to stand *with*, to anchor the intellect in loyalty. To believe is to belong, to place oneself within a circle of commitment, in which sacred narratives and symbols resonate due to their rootedness and continuity. Beliefs differ from theories and opinions in that my beliefs are never merely mine. I cannot hold them at arm's length. As much as I may own them, they own me too. As much as I may shape them, they shape me as well. The search for meaning is not a search for abstract propositions, disembodied truths to which one can assent from an impartial distance. It is the search for a living language of the soul, which flourishes in the soil of tradition and community.

So the tension between faith and skepticism is deeper than their clashing claims. Not only do they teach conflicting truths, but they do so from conflicting psychological positions. At the deepest level, they are at odds in ways that defy our attempts to harmonize their content. Even if we could somehow bring the story of creation into line with Darwin, or square the biblical time line with the evidence of history, that deeper tension would remain. To be a skeptic is to fear emotional engagement as a threat to honest judgment. To find meaning, on the other hand, is to cast one's lot with a tradition and community, to commit to a particular spiritual vocabulary.

The conflict seems intractable. It appears that those who will not choose between the two positions must divide themselves in half. One cannot stand in two places simultaneously. One cannot be loyal and impartial at the same time.

But that is not the final word. In the end, the tension between faith and skepticism proves to be less absolute than we imagined. At a certain point, it becomes possible to have it both ways after all.

That point is where skepticism steps back and becomes skeptical even of itself. At its extreme, skepticism comes to recognize that there is no freedom but the freedom to commit. Freedom that is merely freedom *from*, not *to*, is not freedom at all. Liberty

INTRODUCTION

that forbids loyalty is not liberty but enslavement. Skepticism, at its limit, cannot help but question its own self-sufficiency. It must acknowledge that the sovereign intellect is not as sovereign as it thought.

With that recognition, skepticism evolves into something more expansive, not by undoing itself but by completing itself. It makes room for a new form of faith, not in spite of its own logic but because of it. Doubt becomes a vehicle of commitment. Standing back becomes a mode of standing for and standing with.

The kind of faith that we embrace at that point is not simple, precritical faith, which never knew doubt in the first place. Nor is it reactionary faith, which struggles to suppress our questions. Rather, it is faith with skepticism at its core. It is not the opposite of doubt but its fruition.

All of the eight essays in this book, in some way, touch on the synthesis of detachment and engagement that we reach at the far side of skepticism. Some of the essays describe the journey toward that synthesis. They offer a road map toward the point where separation comes full circle to reintegration, where doubt tips over into affirmation. Others are efforts to exemplify that synthesis, to show how the world looks when we arrive there. Some do a little of both. The essays vary in their content. What unites them is the process that they model or describe, in which skepticism transcends itself. Each is an attempt to reach the point where distance and commitment become one.

The battles that cleave modern society—between science and religion, evidence and authority, liberty and loyalty, autonomy and rootedness—are, at the deepest level, struggles between two versions of the self. On one side is a self that claims to stand alone, and on the other is a self embedded in tradition and community. Our culture wars are ultimately battles over which is more important, to stand back or to stand with. Perhaps, by offering a path beyond that tension, these essays might contribute to the healing of our wounded society.

The sources that I draw on in these essays are mainly from my own tradition, Judaism. But I hope that my interpretations of those sources will be helpful to those of other faiths as well. The struggle to meld spiritual intensity with intellectual integrity, to seek meaning without surrendering autonomy, is one that transcends religious boundaries. These essays are addressed to all who share that struggle.

Overlapping Magisteria

I

From the trial of Galileo to today, science has lived in tension with religion. It might seem that it could not be any other way. Data and equations do not naturally mix with sacred poetry and narrative. Critical detachment cannot easily accommodate allegiance to the teachings of the past. The two modes of thinking seem to be inherently at odds, even within a single mind that values both, let alone across a bitterly divided population prone to culture wars.

Some people who seek peace between the worlds of science and religion make a virtue of their polarization. They argue that the lack of common ground between them is the very thing that rescues them from conflict. Stephen Jay Gould wrote that science and religion can never truly clash because they share no premises. They can never disagree because they have nothing to disagree about. They are "non-overlapping magisteria," neither of which has standing to refute the other's claims.[1]

---

1. Gould, "Non-Overlapping Magisteria."

But I believe that science and religion ought to be at peace with one another because of what they share, not just because of how they differ. In a certain respect, they do overlap.

The kinship that I have in mind has nothing to do with content. It is not due to any similarities in what they teach, such as those between the symbolism of medieval Jewish mysticism and the physics of the big bang.[2] Nor is it due to emotions that we might associate with both, such as the wonder at the natural order that Albert Einstein called the essence of the scientific spirit and the purest distillation of religion.[3] Rather, it is due to a shared impetus that drives both and that keeps both open to new possibilities. We turn to sacred narrative and poetry, as we turn to chemistry and physics, to weave together our experience of the world, to make sense of reality as we perceive it. In contrast to those who define religion as faith in the unseen, I would argue that it is an interpretation of the *seen*.

That is not to say that science and religion deal with the same evidence. Gould was right to draw a line between their purviews. To do otherwise would be to force them into a false competition, which in the end must delegitimize one or the other.

That is what their most rigid partisans do. They pit the two against each other in a contest that their favored side is bound to win. Adversaries of religion argue that religion is no more than a primitive precursor to science which has outlived its usefulness. Now that we know how nature really works, we no longer need faith. Adversaries of science, on the other hand, claim that science is no more than an alternative form of faith which will never match the depth of the real thing. Gould meant to rescue science and religion from such loaded comparisons.

But to spare the two from such polemics need not mean to deny them any commonality at all. The kinship that I am speaking

---

2. For examples of such similarities, see Matt, *God and the Big Bang*.
3. Einstein, "Religion and Science," paras. 7, 12.

of is not about shared subject matter but about a deeper common purpose. Science and religion are related in that they answer the same basic human need: the need to make meaning of experience, albeit different kinds of meaning of different kinds of experience. To serve that purpose, both must be as open-ended as experience itself. Both must evolve in response to new perceptions of the world. In other words, the empiricism at the heart of science extends, in a certain sense, to religion too.

II

To say that faith is empirical, that believing is a response to seeing, requires explanation today, though centuries ago it would not have. The difference is that, for the purpose of gathering evidence about the world, we define seeing more narrowly than we once did. When we speak of evidence today, we tend to limit it to what we see from a specific point of view, one that our ancestors were largely unfamiliar with. We might call it the external point of view, a vantage point detached from our own personhood, which we arrive at by stepping outside ourselves. Today, we privilege the cold eye, which surveys the world as dispassionately as a laboratory sensor.

To such a cold eye, the world is cold as well. From an external vantage point, the world looks very different from the way in which we naturally see it. It appears as nothing more than chemistry and physics, matter and energy governed by natural law. The measurable properties of objects—their size and mass and velocity—appear in sharp relief, while their warmer attributes—their *value*, for example—are invisible. Or, more precisely, such intangible things as value appear as phantoms generated by the central nervous system, shadows cast off by the chemistry and physics of the brain.

At the limit of that outlook, even the subjective self of the observer falls away. The *I* that looks out at the world from that external point of view becomes invisible to itself. Descartes argued that the thing that we know most immediately about the world is the fact of our own subjectivity, our own intangible personhood. We know that we have selves—or rather that we *are* selves—more definitively than we know anything else. We may be mistaken in believing that we have bodies, or even that we have brains, but we cannot be mistaken in believing that there is an *I*, because it takes an *I* to be mistaken.[4]

But to a depersonalized observer detached from his or her own inner life, even that Cartesian certainty falls away. The *I* loses touch with itself. It becomes numb to its own subjectivity. Selfhood disappears, even to itself. It dissolves into the physical workings of the brain, which are explainable by the same laws that govern the rest of nature.

That impersonal way of seeing is what makes science possible. It reveals mathematical relationships among physical entities that were hidden from premodern observers. But as a definition of seeing in general, it is artificially narrow.

Think of what we ordinarily mean by seeing. The world to which we wake up every morning, which we experience with the immediacy of opening our eyes, is a world full of things that cannot be physically quantified. To begin with, it is a world that *matters*, that has value, in a way that its pure physicality cannot explain. Physical facts and processes have no inherent importance. They just *are*. But the world to which we wake up makes a claim on our attention. It evokes wonder. It offers glimpses of the numinous in ways that, from our inner point of view, are irreducible to chemistry and physics. A detached observer might explain away the majesty that we perceive in nature by defining it as an illusion generated by our neurochemistry. But to an engaged observer

---

4. Descartes, *Meditations*, 119–121. Descartes intended his argument to be the first step in a purely rational proof that we have knowledge of the world beyond our own minds. But it also serves as an expression of our most immediate experience.

looking at the world from the perspective of a self, that explanation would entirely miss the point. It would be no more compelling than an effort to explain away the physical existence of the sun by pointing out that our perception of light is neurological as well, or to deny the reality of food by demonstrating that our sense of taste resides within the brain. Just as no amount of neuroscience can erase the rest of what we see from an external point of view, no amount of it can erase what we see just as clearly from an inner point of view—namely, that the world has an inherent grandeur.

The world to which we awaken also contains *selves*—our own and others'—which just as stubbornly resist all efforts to reduce them to the chemistry and physics of our brains.[5] Humanness, observed from its own point of view, transcends its physicality in ways that neuroscience has no language to explain. As human agents, we make moral claims on one another, we wrestle with conflicting values, we make choices, we fall short of our ideals, we struggle to do better. None of that can be reduced to physical law.

To be sure, when viewed from an impersonal distance, personhood and all that goes with it dissolves. Self and other, freedom and responsibility, love and aspiration disappear into their underlying chemistry and physics. The personal becomes impersonal. But viewed from our natural vantage point, personhood and all that it implies has its own irreducible existence. It is as real as any physical fact.

The claim that there is nothing real except what chemistry and physics can account for is called physicalism, or reductive materialism. It is sometimes called scientism as well, in that it makes science the sole arbiter of truth. In recent decades, that philosophy has come to dominate much of the scientific world, and its influence has spread to the general culture as well.[6]

---

5. For a discussion of the logical problems with mind-body reductionism, see Goff, *Galileo's Error*, 53–110.

6. For an extended critique of physicalism in general, see Nagel, *Mind and Cosmos*.

Physicalism starts from an epistemological premise, an assumption about how we know what we know. That premise is that the most accurate observations of the world will always be the most emotionally detached, the most thoroughly drained of everything that makes them human observations. The more we strive to stand outside ourselves, the more clearly we will see reality. If one starts from that premise, then the conclusion that only physical things are real follows naturally. Since the only things that will appear real from a point of view outside the self are those that can be measured spatially and temporally, they must be the only things that *are* real.

Physicalism claims the mantle of empiricism. It declares that only physical evidence can qualify as evidence at all. In other words, it insists that those who draw conclusions about reality from their perception of intangible things—things such as love and value, personhood and freedom—are not really *seeing* at all. They are believing for no good reason, like those who once believed in elves and fairies.

But that is backward. Who is the truer empiricist? Who better exemplifies the openness and curiosity about the world that inspires science at its best? Is it one who rules out much of human experience and declares on pure principle that only one kind of evidence counts? Or is it one who grants the benefit of the doubt to our broadest perception of reality?

We have grown accustomed to assuming that the scientific spirit is inherently reductive. But that is a mistake. Galileo and the other founders of the scientific method in the seventeenth century never claimed that science could explain everything. To be sure, they devoted their energies to understanding what they saw about the world from a detached position. But they never imagined that nothing else exists.[7]

---

7. Galileo and Descartes assigned subjective qualities, such as color and smell, to the realm of the mind, which they considered no less real than the

It seems to me that a truly scientific temperament not only allows us but *requires* us to be open to both kinds of seeing. It has often been noted that there is nothing scientific about scientism. The claim that only things that we can see from an external point of view are real is not a claim that can be tested in the laboratory. But the point goes deeper. It is not only that scientism is unscientific but that it is *anti*-scientific. Its sensibility and method are inimical to those of science. Scientific skepticism is, above all, skepticism toward dogmatic claims untested by experience. The essence of the scientific method is to give priority to evidence over theory.[8] To be sure, the method takes into account that our eyes can lie. But when experience and theory conflict, science always breaks the tie with more experience. It never allows theory on its own to override what we observe.

Scientism reasons in the opposite direction. It starts with the a priori claim that the only things that are real are those that we can see from an impersonal perspective and rejects all evidence to the contrary. It writes off as unreliable everything that we perceive from the perspective of the self, and does so by pure fiat. But, if we are committed to putting experience first, how can we dismiss perceptions of reality that seem irreducibly true simply on the basis of an arbitrary preference for one point of view over another? To reject experiential evidence for no reason except prejudice against its source is not skepticism but dogmatism.

An authentic scientific temperament, then, must respect the raw material that motivates religious searching. It must be receptive to experiences of the numinous, of value, of personhood and freedom, of self-transcendence and the pull of moral obligation. A

---

physical world (Nagel, *Mind and Cosmos*, 35; Goff, *Galileo's Error*, 21).

8. I do not mean to suggest that science is entirely empirical, with no a priori premises. The most basic scientific assumption of all—that nature will follow the same laws tomorrow that it follows today—is not subject to empirical proof. My point is that science does not allow such premises, on their own, to overturn empirical data.

true commitment to empiricism requires us to be open to whatever we perceive about reality, from wherever we perceive it. To be sure, a scientific mind will not readily assign what it perceives from the inside to an entirely separate realm, a domain of the spirit. It will resist a dualistic worldview. But much religious thought resists dualism too. To be true to our experience, we need only grant that the world is more complex than the reductive impulse would allow. There is more to reality than we can see from any single vantage point.[9]

So we can say this much at least: the scientific spirit at its most authentic validates religious *questions*. Why? Because religious questions are responses to a kind of seeing—in fact, a kind of seeing that is more immediate than that which gives rise to science itself. The empiricism at the heart of science tells us that the questions that we ask about what we perceive specifically as human beings are real questions after all.

III

But does the kinship between science and religion extend further? Does the spirit of empiricism validate the search for religious *answers* as well? Does it sanction the work of weaving sacred narratives and constructing theologies, systems of meaning that cannot be tested from the outside?

I believe that it does. In fact, I believe that a true commitment to empiricism not only validates that work but requires some version of it. The same sensibility that pushes us toward the use of mathematical equations to make sense of what we see from an external point of view pushes us toward the use of sacred poetry—or

---

9. Dual-aspect theorists argue that to see our own nature in full requires two points of view, the view from inside and the view from outside (Nagel, *View from Nowhere*, 28–32). Panpsychists such as Philip Goff generalize that idea and argue that consciousness as an intrinsic feature of all matter (see Goff, *Galileo's Error*).

some secular derivative of it—to make a different kind of sense of that which we perceive about the world from the inside.

Let me explain by fleshing out the implications of empiricism. If empiricism is a commitment to be guided by what we perceive, then one of its implications—as we have seen—is that we must not favor certain types of evidence over others based on a priori preferences. But there is a second implication of the definition, specifically the part about being *guided* by experience. It is that we must make some effort to interpret what we see, to make sense of it. Without some attempt to contextualize what we perceive, we cannot be guided by it. Raw observations have no meaning on their own. They take on meaning only as we organize them into a conceptual scheme.

Science weaves together things that we perceive from an external point of view. It constructs theories to explain how those observations relate to one another, which we can then test from the same impersonal perspective. But, if we were to stop there—if we were to limit ourselves to scientific answers in our search for meaning and coherence on the grounds that only those answers can be externally tested—we would be violating the first implication of our definition. We would be making a decision to be guided by just one type of data, and we would be doing so based on nothing but an arbitrary preference for one point of view over another. We would be declaring that what we see from the inside, simply because it cannot be reduced to mathematical equations, is unworthy of our work of meaning making and must be relegated to the realm of unintelligible noise. In other words, we would be elevating ideology above experience. In doing so, we would be placing ourselves squarely in the anti-empiricist camp.

So empiricism, broadly understood, must be a commitment to interpret what we see *on its own terms*, to recognize that different kinds of data call for different modes of comprehension. To interpret our experience evenhandedly means to grant that we must process different kinds of information differently, in ways consistent with the nature of the information. Making sense means different things from different perspectives. Hence, a commitment to be guided by experience requires openness to different understandings of what kind of sense we ought to try to make of things. If empiricism calls on us to interpret external information from the outside in the language of impersonal equations, it also calls on us to interpret internal information from the inside, to make the things that we perceive specifically as selves intelligible to ourselves.

When we struggle to construct that latter kind of meaning, we inevitably turn to language that is more like poetry than mathematics, language that lives within a specific culture, that speaks with the warmth of particularity. We have no choice but to express ourselves as cultural beings, since, in our personhood, we can be nothing else. The subjective self is embedded in its time and place, framed by its allegiances, rooted in its history. The *I* finds form and substance in a *we*. Hence, its natural vocabulary is specific rather than general, concrete rather than abstract, engaged rather than detached. It speaks through narratives and metaphors that resonate by virtue of their rootedness in a tradition and community. In that respect, the language of the searching self—even in its secular dialects—is always something like religious language.

That is what I mean when I say that the logic of empiricism, the same logic that drives our search for scientific understanding, pushes us toward the use of sacred language to make inner sense of what we see from the inside, to interpret things that we know but cannot prove, things that we perceive but cannot measure.

IV

I have argued that the empiricism at the heart of science motivates and validates religious searching too. But when I said at the outset that science and religion ought to honor one another due to what they share, that was only half of what I meant. I believe that religion, at its most authentic, also pushes us to honor science. If the ethic at the heart of science challenges us to take religion seriously, then the reverse is true as well. If religion is a response to our experience of the world, it can succeed in making meaning only if it evolves with new perceptions of reality. If the capacity to take in new information is part of what makes religion what it is, then religion's own integrity demands that it take science seriously. For its own sake, religion must cede ownership of the external point of view to science.

To be sure, in this era of reactionary backlash, religion frequently does the opposite. Anti-modern strands of faith push back against the sciences. They treat sacred narratives as quasi-scientific claims about the world, as refutations of geology and biology.

But the insistence that religious faith provides the kind of knowledge that can refute science is not a feature of faith in general. To the contrary, religious fundamentalism as we know it is a recent innovation. Before modernity, when religion had less to be defensive about, it rarely made such quasi-scientific claims about the world.

Consider, for example, biblical narratives. When the Bible tells us that such and such a thing happened, we often assume that its purpose was to give us the kind of information that we today would turn to science or history to provide. But the actual character of the narratives belies that assumption. Biblical stories are not anything like what we would expect of an attempt to nail down external facts. They are full of loose ends. They contradict themselves without apology. They ignore questions that a scientist or historian would consider crucial and concern themselves with claims that would have been impossible to check externally, even by one who was there at the time. All of this suggests that their purpose was never to tell us what a dispassionate observer would have seen. It was to paint a picture of reality according to what we today would call the inner point of view.

We can say the same about most premodern systems of theology. To the extent that ancient and medieval theologians made seemingly objective claims about reality—such as the claim that God treats people fairly—they generally did so in a way that was impossible to falsify externally. In response to contrary evidence, they would stretch and adapt their claims such that they could never be refuted from the outside. That is because external facts were never the main thing that they were trying to account for. They were describing the world as it appeared to them from the inside, as meaning-seeking human beings. The question that is so important to us—What can we accurately say about external facts?—was not their question.

It was not their question because they did not distinguish as sharply as we do between the external and internal points of view in the first place. They did not yet have the kind of modern selves that strive to step back from their natural vantage point and see the world from a detached position. The objective point of view as we know it, a perspective that aspires to exclude the viewer's personhood, did not yet exist.

The core dilemma that religion faces in our time is to choose what to do about a way of seeing that did not exist until modernity. For most of human history, religion could claim jurisdiction over all that we perceived, and it could do so honestly. Impersonal investigation was no threat to faith, because the self had not asserted the degree of psychological distance that would make such inquiry possible. But today, if religion wishes to claim ownership of all that we see, it must close off access to a point of view with which we have become familiar, that of the external observer. It must insist that there is nothing to be seen at all except from the perspective of a believing self.

Alternatively, religion can give up its claim to comprehensiveness. It can admit that it no longer owns all points of view, that there are types of information that it lacks the tools to interpret.

It seems to me that the alternative that requires less repudiation of the past is to choose honesty over comprehensiveness. Religion that is less than all-encompassing is still recognizably itself. But religion that demands that we deny all other ways of seeing is distorted beyond recognition. If religion is to retain its reason for being today, I believe that it must give up its claim to own all that we see. And to make that choice—to renounce what it cannot interpret for the sake of what it can—leads naturally to honoring science as a complementary endeavor. The self-limitation that makes religion relevant today also makes science necessary.

Hence, religion at its best affirms the work of science, just as science at its best affirms religion. The integrity that makes religion matter pushes it to honor scientific inquiry, just as the scientific spirit validates religious searching. The line that we have drawn between their jurisdictions—between the inner and the outer points of view—is not an arbitrary truce line between adversaries. Nor is it an impenetrable wall between two worlds that know nothing of each other. Rather, it is a division of labor that honors the essential character of each type of work and is sanctioned and supported by the best in each. The core values of science and religion point toward the same partnership. More broadly, they point toward a middle ground in our culture wars, a place of modesty and moderation in a world torn by extremes.

Dover Beach

∼

I

On their honeymoon in 1851, Matthew Arnold and his wife, Frances, spent a night in Dover, overlooking the English Channel. Later, Arnold made that place the setting of his poem "Dover Beach," a meditation on the search for meaning in a world without religious faith. In the poem, Arnold laments the scientific skepticism that has left him spiritually bereft and looks for solace in love.

As the poem opens, it is nighttime. Arnold, as he poetically portrays himself, looks down from the window of the room where he and his wife are staying. Below him is Dover Beach, which, in his imagination, represents the modern world. It is a world darkened by religious doubt, stripped of spiritual significance. The breaking of the waves against the sand conveys the tedium of life without a higher purpose.

> Listen! You hear the grating roar
> Of pebbles which the waves draw back, and fling,
> At their return, up the high strand,
> Begin, and cease, and then again begin,

Dover Beach

> With tremulous cadence slow, and bring
> The eternal note of sadness in.[1]

The poet nostalgically recalls a different sea, the sea of faith, whose high tide once filled the world with sanctity. That older sea has receded, leaving the world empty and exposed. All that the poet sees below him now is cold matter driven by impersonal, amoral forces.

> The Sea of Faith
> Was once, too, at the full, and round earth's shore
> Lay like the folds of a bright girdle furled.
> But now I only hear
> Its melancholy, long, withdrawing roar,
> Retreating, to the breath
> Of the night-wind, down the vast edges drear
> And naked shingles of the world.[2]

In a world devoid of meaning, emptied of its sanctity by science, the poet hopes that love might offer consolation. So he affirms his commitment to his wife and asks her to do the same. He seeks in love what he cannot find in faith.

> Ah, love, let us be true
> To one another! for the world, which seems
> To lie before us like a land of dreams,
> So various, so beautiful, so new,
> Hath really neither joy, nor love, nor light,
> Nor certitude, nor peace, nor help for pain;
> And we are here as on a darkling plain
> Swept with confused alarms of struggle and flight,
> Where ignorant armies clash by night.[3]

But at the heart of the poet's hope in the preceding passage is a contradiction. Having just staked everything on love, the poet goes on to complain that there is no such thing as love. He declares

---

1. Arnold, "Dover Beach," lines 9–14.
2. Arnold, "Dover Beach," lines 21–28.
3. Arnold, "Dover Beach," lines 28–37.

that the very thing in which he hopes to find comfort is absent from the world.

Let me repeat that part of the preceding passage:

> The world, which seems
> To lie before us like a land of dreams,
> So various, so beautiful, so new,
> Hath really neither joy, nor *love*, nor light,
> Nor certitude, nor peace, nor help for pain.[4]

If there is really no love in the world, nor any possibility of joy or light or certitude or peace or help for pain, what is the poet reaching for as he says to his wife, "Ah, love, let us be true / To one another!"? Why seek comfort in what he himself declares does not exist?

Perhaps his point is that, although the world outside their window is meaningless and empty, their marriage might be different. Though there is no love *out there* on the "naked shingles of the world," there might still be love *in here*, in the room that he and his wife share.

But how can what is *in here* be entirely separate from what is *out there*? Their room, after all, is part of the world. The universe that the poet surveys from his window includes him and his wife, and all that is between them. If love is real enough to bring him comfort for his lack of faith, how can it be absent from the world as a whole? On the other hand, if love is nothing more than an illusion—if it is not part of the world—what is the point of searching for it in his marriage?

We might write off the contradiction as a matter of hyperbole. Perhaps, when the poet declares that "the world . . . hath neither joy nor love," he means only that the world is not *inherently* a world of love. Yes, love might happen to exist. We might find it here and there. But love is not intrinsic to reality, not part of the essential makeup of the universe. Love is a fragmentary fact, a

---

4. Arnold, "Dover Beach," lines 29–33; emphasis mine.

random phenomenon detached from any greater source, like the twitching of a severed nerve. It is an accident, a manifestation of the chaos, not an answer to it.

But if that is what the poet means when he declares that the world is loveless, what sense does it make for him to turn to love for comfort? If love has no larger significance, what spiritual consolation can it offer? If it tells us nothing about reality as a whole, how can it mitigate the meaninglessness of the universe?

To be sure, even if love means nothing, it might still serve as a diversion, a momentary source of pleasure. There is a long tradition in Western literature of the jaded roué who turns to love for fleeting relief in an indifferent universe. Consider, for example, Andrew Marvell's "To His Coy Mistress," in which the poet appeals to his reluctant lover in that spirit.

> And yonder all before us lie
> Deserts of vast eternity....
> The grave's a fine and private place,
> But none, I think, do there embrace....
> Now let us sport us while we may...[5]

But "sport" is not what Arnold seems to have in mind at all in "Dover Beach." His tone is nothing like Marvell's. Arnold's voice is one of hope, not despair, of earnest longing, not cynical defiance. His words to his wife—"Ah, love, let us be true / To one another!"—express a yearning for constancy, not for momentary pleasure. Far from conceding the vanity of life, the poet does the opposite. He reaches for a higher purpose, a form of secular salvation. He seeks a source of meaning on the human plane that can make up for what is missing in the cosmos as a whole.

But how can love be that source of meaning, that fixed point of reference, if it signifies nothing beyond itself? We cannot order our lives around an accident. We cannot navigate by a lightning

---

5. Marvell, "To His Coy Mistress," 23–24, 31–32, 37.

strike. If love points nowhere, if it tells us nothing about reality in general, how can it serve as our North Star?

The only way in which we can resolve the contradiction is to posit that the poet *does* believe, in spite of himself. Without acknowledging it, he expresses an implicit faith. Even in the midst of what he calls despair, he still intuits that love points beyond itself, that it offers a glimpse of a transcendent order. Otherwise, his appeal to his wife would be a non sequitur. His words to her would be no answer at all to the emptiness that he sees outside the window. That love *is* his answer to that emptiness tells us that he recognizes love not as a cosmic accident but as a sign of something stable on which he might build his life. The poet turns to love in search of meaning in a world that he insists is desolate. But if love can make life meaningful, the world is not entirely desolate after all. In his appeal to his wife, he implicitly affirms that faith, even as he claims that he has none.

II

Arnold, as he portrayed himself in "Dover Beach," reminds me of a type of spiritual searcher that we often see today. In synagogues that I have known, I have met many people who embody the same contradiction. They yearn for an authentic bond with other human beings, past and present—not to make it possible to live their faith but to fill the void left by the lack of it, to anchor themselves in an indifferent universe. They insist that they are unbelievers, that no faith motivates their search. Yet they turn to spiritual community in the hope of finding—if not certitude—then perhaps joy, and light, and love, and peace, and help for pain.

Notwithstanding all their protests, that makes them believers after all. If it were not for an implicit faith that drives their search, their yearning for community would make no sense. If the universe were as cold and mechanistic as they suggest, what spiritual solace could community provide? If love meant nothing in the larger scheme of things, the solidarity that they seek would be a cosmic anomaly which manifests no greater order. But in that case, if that solidarity pointed to nothing but itself, how could it serve to orient them in the world? In the end, there can be no meaning in the room if there is none outside it.

Like Arnold's poetic persona, those searchers bifurcate between the specific and the general. They seek solace in particular relationships even as they claim to seek no solace in the cosmos as a whole. But if their universe were actually as indifferent as they claim it is, their efforts would be pointless. What exists in here can bring us no redemption if it points to nothing out there. There can be no spiritual consolation in pure chance.

Hence, it appears that they believe in more than they acknowledge. Contrary to their words, they must hold that human love provides a glimpse of something greater, even if that something remains vague. For whatever reason, they cannot express what actually motivates them. They cannot articulate their deepest intuition, even to themselves.

III

The contradiction at the heart of "Dover Beach" and in the words of the conflicted searchers that I have encountered is an extreme expression of a tension at the heart of modern culture as a whole. By highlighting that tension, those examples illustrate the norm.

As creatures of modernity, we struggle with a gap between our deepest motivations and the language that we speak. Everyone lives for something. To imagine otherwise is to be naïve about the purity of doubt. But often, we cannot say what that something is. Our secular vocabulary, drained of sacred metaphors and symbols, cannot do justice to what we implicitly believe.

For most of us, that implicit faith is manifest in our relationships with other people. The evidence of our own lives tells us so. Despite our skepticism, we still orient ourselves by love. We still organize our lives around empathy. Were it not for the implicit faith that love has meaning, that it transcends randomness, we would not persist in navigating by its light. That we still treat love as a beacon in an otherwise indifferent world is evidence that, even now, we tacitly believe that it points toward a greater order.

But we are hard-pressed to express that faith, or even to acknowledge that it is a faith at all. Like Arnold, we suffer from a misalignment between our deepest motives and our words. We find it hard to say what is in our hearts.

That is the toll of modernity. The language that we speak most fluently, that of secular skepticism, cannot express the truths that anchor us and shape our actions. Stripped of sacred poetry, that language lacks the power to convey our deepest insights. On the other hand, the language of the sacred, which *could* express those insights, is one that we speak haltingly. Having banished that language to heaven long ago, we feel little liberty to draw on it to make sense of our lives on earth today. Having written off its metaphors as false, we feel that we have no right to turn back to them to say what we experience as true.

In other words, the spiritual crisis of modernity is not what Arnold imagined it to be. Arnold thought that existential despair was the inevitable result of intellectual honesty. He located his dilemma in his inability to believe what his ancestors had believed and his unwillingness to pretend otherwise. He assumed that, short of betraying what modernity had made him, he had no path to faith. But in framing the problem in that way, he overlooked the faith that he still had, which was no farther from him than his own capacity to state it.

Often, we make the same mistake. We imagine that in order to believe, we must surrender our capacity to doubt. We must squeeze ourselves into a world of faith that has no room for who we actually are. But that is a misreading of the problem. What we truly suffer from is not the lack of other people's truths but the inability to state our own. What we miss is not the faith that we abandoned long ago but the means to live by that which we still have. To believe, we need not forfeit our integrity. We need not sacrifice the skepticism that has set us free. To the contrary, our challenge is to do the opposite, to seize *more* freedom so that we can be still truer to ourselves, to push our intellectual integrity even further, to the point where it no longer forces us to contradict ourselves. To confess a faith need only mean to claim the liberty to put our deepest, most elusive intuitions into words.

IV

In his interpretation of the Golden Rule—"You shall love your neighbor as yourself; I am the Lord"[6]—Martin Buber offered a model of such liberation. He turned to the Hasidic literature of the eighteenth century in search of a vocabulary that could express what Arnold had no words to say—namely, that human love, as we experience it, is a window to a larger order. Drawing on that mystical literature, Buber called our love of other human beings a revelation of God's love, an opening to the transcendent.

> The true meaning of love of one's neighbor is not that it is a command from God which we are to fulfill, but that through it and in it we meet God. This is shown in the interpretation of this command. It is not just written, "Love thy neighbor as thyself," as though the sentence ended there, but it goes on: "Love thy neighbor as thyself, I am the Lord" (Leviticus 19:18). The grammatical construction of the original text shows quite clearly that the meaning is: You shall deal lovingly with your "neighbor,"

---

6. Lev 19:18. Throughout this book, translations of biblical, rabbinic, and liturgical texts are my own, unless otherwise noted.

that is, with everyone you meet along life's road, and you shall deal with him as one equal to yourself. The second part, however, adds, "I am the Lord"—and here the hasidic interpretation comes in: "You think I am far away from you, but in your love for your neighbor you will find Me; not in his love for you but in yours for him." He who loves brings God and the world together.[7]

In teaching that our love of neighbor offers us a glimpse of the divine, Buber was not beckoning us backward. He was not urging us to suppress our doubts, to force ourselves into an ancient world of faith. The belief that he proposed was not the kind that limits what we see, that constricts our vision of the world. Rather, what he offered was a language that has the capacity to name what we experience every day but would otherwise lack words to express.

That we persist in grounding our lives in empathy, that we find meaning by honoring the otherness of those around us, is evidence that we experience our own love as a visible thread of a hidden tapestry, as a pointer toward an elusive absolute, a cosmic constant. If we did not implicitly believe that our love manifests a quality that pervades reality, we could not orient our lives by it. To call that hidden constant by a sacred name, as Buber did, is not to limit our horizons but to claim a new degree of freedom.[8]

The work of making meaning in the world begins with the liberation of our speech. It starts not *out there* but *in here*, when we dare to give a name to that which motivates our actions. We turn to the past not to escape the skepticism of the present but to find a way to say what intellectual integrity, even now, compels us to affirm.

---

7. Buber, "Silent Question," 212.

8. The divine name that appears in Lev 19:18 is the tetragrammaton YHWH, which Jewish tradition treats as unpronounceable (it is usually translated "Lord," in keeping with the Hebrew euphemism *Adonai*). The tetragrammaton appears to be a permutation of the Hebrew verb "to be." Hence, Arthur Green and others understand it to refer to being itself, the ground of all existence (see Green, *Radical Judaism*, 16–33).

Consciousness of Consciousness

∼

I

Modeh Ani ("I Give Thanks") is the first prayer that the Jewish liturgy provides for us to say upon awakening in the morning. The prayer expresses gratitude for the renewal of consciousness:

> I give thanks to you,
> Living and enduring King,
> You who have restored my life to me in mercy.
> Great is your faithfulness.

The prayer is short—just twelve Hebrew words (which translate to twenty-three in English). But if we compare Modeh Ani to the blessings of thanksgiving that the Jewish liturgy prescribes for other ordinary gifts, we might wonder why it is not even shorter. When we express gratitude for the foods that we eat, the sights and smells that we experience, the sacred deeds that we have the opportunity to perform, we do so even more concisely. For example, we do not bother to point out that the gift of bread is an expression of God's mercy. We simply say:

> Blessed are you, Lord our God,
> King of the universe,
> Who brings forth bread from the earth.

We state the fact as we understand it and trust that that is sufficient. To belabor the point, to explain that God's bringing forth bread from the earth is an act of mercy, would be to say too much. The premise of the blessing over bread, and of the many other blessings of thanksgiving that are built on the same template, is a confident one. It is that even ordinary facts are wondrous enough to evoke awe and gratitude if we just pay attention. Everyday miracles do not need to be explicated. They just need to be noticed and appreciated.

So why does Modeh Ani not treat our awakening in the same way—as a fact whose plain extraordinariness requires no commentary? Why insist on explaining that the renewal of our consciousness manifests a particular divine attribute—namely, mercy?

Not only does the invocation of God's mercy seem superfluous here, but it threatens to obscure the main point of the prayer, and to do so in particularly troubling ways. Mercy implies a singling out for special leniency, a bending of the norm. By definition, mercy cannot be for everyone. If it were, it would not be mercy but the norm itself. So what does Modeh Ani mean by calling my awakening a gift of mercy?

Does it mean to say that, rightfully, I should have died in my sleep last night, but that God graciously bent justice in my favor? If so, what does the prayer imply about all those who did not wake up this morning?—that they got what they deserved? Or does the prayer mean to say that *no one* deserved to awaken to another day this morning, but that some of us were blessed to do so anyway? In that case, why should I be one of the elect?

Those questions are difficult and troubling. Moreover, they appear to be beside the point. So why does the prayer go out of its way to raise them when it would be simpler just to say thank you? To express gratitude, we need not bring up the question of what we do or do not deserve. We need only acknowledge what we have. If we can thank God for bread, and for a hundred other gifts, without defining them specifically as acts of mercy, why speak of mercy here? Would the prayer not be better off without that extra language?

The problem of saying too much does not end there. The prayer's closing phrase also seems, at best, superfluous. The words "Great is your faithfulness" suggest that my awakening this morning was not only a miracle but a miracle that, in some sense, I could count on. The phrase comes from the book of Lamentations:

> But this I take to heart,
> And therefore do I hope.
> The Lord's kindnesses are not exhausted,
> [God's] mercies are not spent.
> They are renewed each morning.
> *Great is your faithfulness.*
> "The Lord is my portion," my soul declares;
> Therefore will I hope . . . .[1]

In their original context, those words were a call for hope in the aftermath of the destruction of Jerusalem, when all seemed lost. Transplanted to this daily prayer, the phrase no longer serves as a response to a particular catastrophe but as an answer to the tenuousness of life in general. It reminds us that as fragile as the gift of consciousness is, it is not as fragile as it might be. In spite of everything, life has a resilience, and that resilience is not an accident. For however many mornings I am privileged to wake up, I do so because life is a persistent gift.

But again, we do not embellish other prayers of thanksgiving in that way. When we thank God for bread, for instance, we do not speak of how reliable that gift is. We refer to the immediate fact in front of us: that we have bread to eat, which wondrously comes

---

1. Lam 3:23, italics added.

from the earth. We do not up the ante by declaring that the gift of bread is one in which we can have confidence. We speak of what we witness here and now, and leave it at that.

That restraint, that narrow focus on what is concrete and immediate, is exactly what we would expect in an expression of pure gratitude. To be grateful is to appreciate the gift that is before us in the present moment, not to reflect on how likely it was that we would receive it. It is to give thanks for a particular thing, not to contemplate the odds of that thing recurring.

Moreover, to refer to God's dependability not only distracts from simple gratitude but potentially conflicts with it. Not only are gratitude and confidence not the same thing, but they are often opposites. Too much trust in the reliability of our gifts can short-circuit gratitude. It can drain blessings of their miraculous character. It can transform wonder into complacency, gifts into givens. To be sure, we need not push our confidence to that extreme. But even short of that, to speak at all of God's dependability diverts our attention from the particularity of the present moment, which is the only place where gratitude can truly live. It moves us from the concrete realm of experience to an abstract realm of generalization.

So why does Modeh Ani say what seems, in two respects, to be too much? Why speak of mercy on the one hand and dependability on the other if what we really mean to say is something simpler: that we are grateful to be awake again? If the blessings that the Jewish liturgy prescribes for other gifts do not require that extra language, why does this prayer need it?

II

Perhaps the reason why Modeh Ani requires that extra language is that consciousness is unlike other gifts. To summon gratitude for the renewal of awareness is harder than it is to summon gratitude for other things. It requires extra rhetorical help.

Consciousness of Consciousness

Part of the problem is that consciousness is easier to take for granted than most other gifts. In fact, it is almost impossible not to take it for granted. Simply to state that we woke up this morning will rarely be enough to break through our complacency, because to say that we are conscious is to say something so obvious that it could not be otherwise.

Consciousness differs from all other things that we possess in that we can never be aware of lacking it. True, we can imagine not having awakened this morning. We can envision ourselves dead or comatose. But to do so, we must adopt the point of view of someone other than ourselves, or that of no one in particular. We must step back from the very self that would give thanks, the self that is experiencing awareness in the first place, to a vantage point other than our own.

But the effect of stepping back in that way is to drain our gratitude of its immediacy. That is the bind. We can contemplate not being conscious or we can inhabit the self that *is* conscious, but it is difficult to do both at the same time. To be grateful means not to take our gifts as givens. But insofar as we experience anything at all from our first-person point of view, consciousness *is*, in fact, a given. Hence, gratitude for consciousness is a unique challenge.

Could it be in order to break through that bind that Modeh Ani ratchets up its language and insists that our awakening each morning is an expression of God's mercy, a bending of the norm? Perhaps the prayer exaggerates the point in order to shake us into seeing what is so difficult for us to see: that the essential given of all human experience is not a given at all. Perhaps the prayer goes out on a rhetorical limb, even to the point of declaring that awareness is a special dispensation, because otherwise, we would not notice being awake all.

If so, that strategy addresses only half the problem. Mixed with our complacency is fear. If we take consciousness for granted, it is not only because we cannot easily do otherwise but also because we do not *want* to do otherwise. Not only do we naturally fail to recognize that awareness is a gift, but we go out of our way to avoid that insight. To do anything else would mean to recognize how fragile life is. It would mean to realize that had circumstances been only slightly different, we would not have awakened this morning. We do not admit that readily. Most likely, we do not admit it at all without some reassurance. To be grateful for being awake is, at the same time, to face a fundamental fear.

Perhaps that is why Modeh Ani ends with the words "Great is your faithfulness." If we are to face the fragility of our lives, we need some sense of constancy. Having pushed us to confront our vulnerability, perhaps the prayer goes on to speak of God's reliability in order to reassure us—even at the risk of catering to the very complacency that it has just attempted to dispel—that the gift of consciousness is not a capricious gift. As fragile as awareness is, it is not an accident. True, we cannot count on waking up each day. More than that, we *should* not count on it. But we should not discount life's resilience either. Having shaken our complacency by defining our awareness as an exception to the norm, Modeh Ani then turns around and comforts us as we face our insecurity. In speaking of God's faithfulness, it reassures us that consciousness is not a random fact—that it manifests a deeper order.

By invoking opposites, mercy and dependability, Modeh Ani pushes us and pulls us at the same time. It dispels complacency and denies chaos. It challenges and reassures. It disrupts and comforts. It shakes and soothes. In the elusive space in which that push and pull are in accord, Modeh Ani awakens consciousness of consciousness.

III

In the philosophy of mind, the central puzzle—the mind-body problem—concerns the nature of consciousness. The question is this: What is the relationship between mind and brain? What is the connection between awareness—the experience of being a *person*, a subjective self—and the impersonal chemical processes within the brain that correlate with that experience?

The prevailing view today, called physicalism (or reductive materialism) is that mind and brain are identical. There can be nothing to the former but the latter, since only physical things are ultimately real. Consciousness is nothing more than the fact of having a brain. In much of the scientific world, that theory is accepted as a given, a self-evident fact.

On the other side of the debate are a variety of critics of physicalism, both secular and religious. The philosopher Thomas Nagel, who challenges physicalism from an atheistic position, is a leader of that opposition.

Many opponents of physicalism concede that mind and brain are *inextricable*, that the former cannot exist without the latter. But all insist that the equation "Mind = Brain" is logically untenable. There is something on the left side of the equal sign that is not on the right—namely, our *personhood*, our experience of having a subjective point of view, of being a self, which is invisible to neuroscience.[2] Mind and brain may be two manifestations of some mysterious third thing which we do not yet understand. But they are not identical to each other.

Physicalists accuse their critics of seeing mystery where there is none. True, they say, we do not yet have a complete scientific theory of consciousness. But there is nothing about consciousness that we lack the tools to explain. Like everything else in nature, it is reducible to chemistry and physics. It is governed by the same laws that control all of reality. Hence, if we could get the science right, we could predict our inner stream of consciousness in the same way that we know that warm air will rise and that water will flow downhill. There is a physical inevitability to our inner life.

2. Nagel, *Mind and Cosmos*, 40–41.

Moreover, physicalists insist that the origin of consciousness is no mystery either.

At that level, it is not inevitability that dispels the mystery but accident. Originally, like every other part of our biology, consciousness emerged as a random mutation. Perhaps it spread genetically because it offered some advantage in the struggle for survival. Or perhaps it was a by-product of some other adaptive trait, and so persisted by association. In either case, consciousness at first appeared for no reason at all.

Critics of physicalism reply that neither claim—that our stream of consciousness is scientifically predictable or that the origin of consciousness was accidental—dispels the mystery. First, to reduce consciousness to chemistry and physics does not explain our inner life at all but instead explains it away. The answer leaves out the very thing that calls for explanation to begin with. It does not even touch on the reality of consciousness as we experience it, the fact that there is a subjective *I* that asks the question in the first place. Secondly, to call the origin of consciousness an accident is no explanation either. It is a denial of the need for explanation, an intellectual abdication. Instead of an answer, it is a dismissal of the question. Our sense that the origin of consciousness requires an explanation cannot be banished by pure fiat.

For those who push back against physicalism, who insist that the mystery of consciousness cannot be disposed of so easily, Modeh Ani offers a poetry of protest. First, the prayer provides a language of resistance to the intellectual complacency that would turn our inner life into a given, just one more chemical and physical inevitability. It does so by insisting that we speak of consciousness as *mercy*, an exception to the rule, a bending of the law. Through that language, Modeh Ani gives voice to our insistence that our personhood, our subjectivity, will never be explained by the impersonal laws that govern energy and matter. Awareness is a mystery to notice, a wonder to take seriously.

In the next breath, Modeh Ani offers us a language of resistance to the notion that our inner life arose as the result of a pure accident. It does so by insisting that awareness is *dependable*—that in some mysterious way, its emergence in nature was something that could be expected. With the phrase "Great is your faithfulness," the prayer expresses our rejection of the claim that mere chance is sufficient to explain the origin of consciousness. It gives voice to our intuition that consciousness is not a random, fragmentary fact with no connection to a larger order but a product of some hidden tendency inherent in the evolutionary process. As Thomas Nagel wrote:

> The existence of consciousness is both one of the most familiar and one of the most astounding things about the world. No conception of the natural order that does not reveal it as something to be expected can aspire even to the outline of completeness.[3]

When it comes to the philosophy of mind, Modeh Ani offers little in the way of explanation. But it can serve as an expression of skepticism toward the reigning orthodoxy, a refusal to submit to answers that are not really answers.

IV

Among Jewish prayers of gratitude, Modeh Ani stands out due to its extra language—namely, that of mercy and dependability. The prayer requires extra words because it has greater obstacles to overcome. To awaken us to the gift of being awake, the prayer must go to extraordinary lengths to challenge us on the one hand and to reassure us on the other.

---

3. Nagel, *Mind and Cosmos*, 53. Nagel makes the case that consciousness cannot be the result of purely physical and chemical processes as we currently understand them. Hence, there must be an unrecognized bias toward consciousness in nature.

But the obstacles to which the prayer responds are not essentially different from the obstacles that stand in the way of other kinds of gratitude. They differ in degree, not in kind. The work of being grateful for the gift of consciousness is just an especially challenging version of the work of being grateful in general.

To be grateful is to overcome complacency, our sense that things could not be otherwise. It is to cultivate surprise. But it is also the opposite: to see consistency in things that otherwise might seem capricious, to cultivate confidence. We are not grateful for things that seem inevitable, entirely predictable. Neither are we grateful for things that seem completely random, accidental.

Gratitude lives where two apparent opposites, surprise and confidence, overlap. To be grateful is to wonder at things that otherwise might seem routine while trusting that those things are not matters of pure chance. It is to acknowledge that our gifts are far from givens, even as we glimpse behind those gifts—even our most tenuous and fragile gifts—a mysterious bias toward blessing.

The Jewish prayer of gratitude for consciousness, in its emphatic way, shows us the tension in which all gratitude lives. It reminds us that the things that we take most for granted are contingent, and that the things that we are most afraid of losing have a deeper constancy behind them.

The very language that makes this prayer exceptional, the language of mercy and dependability, clarifies the rule. It teaches us the key ingredients of gratitude in general. The first prayer of thanksgiving in our daily liturgy defines, in sharp relief, the quality that much of the rest of the liturgy attempts to cultivate. It shines light on what is perhaps the most important goal of all prayer: the synthesis of surprise and confidence that unlocks the human heart.

The Exile of Language

∾

The Lord said to Moses: "Go and tell Pharaoh, king of Egypt, to let the Israelites leave his land." But Moses replied to the Lord: "See, even the Israelites will not listen to me. How, then, will Pharaoh listen to me, a man of uncircumcised lips?"[1]

I

What prevented Moses from making himself heard? In what sense were his lips uncircumcised?

According to the *Zohar*, the classic text of the medieval Jewish mystical tradition known as kabbalah, the problem was not really Moses's at all.[2] His inability to speak was not a private defect but a symptom of a cosmic disorder.

The authors of the *Zohar* believed that what occurs on earth—for good or ill—is the result of complex interactions within the divine realm. As God's energy flows downward toward our world, it

---

1. Exod 6:10–12.

2. Kabbalah ("that which is received") originated in the twelfth century and flowered in the centuries that followed. The *Zohar* (the "Book of Radiance") was the work of a school of Castilian kabbalists who lived in the late thirteenth century.

must pass through a variety of portals which are aspects of divinity itself. The interplay among those facets of God's inner life—their push and pull, their alignments and misalignments—determines how, and in what form, that divine energy reaches us. What happens here is a reflection of those processes above.

So why was Moses tongue-tied? According to the *Zohar*, it was because God, in a sense, was tongue-tied too. Moses's muteness was a symptom of God's muteness. Due to a misalignment of two aspects of divinity—Voice and Articulation—two portals that control the downward flow of divine energy, God's speech had been cut off. Language was in exile from its source of meaning. Hence, Moses could not prophesy.[3]

To understand this diagnosis of the problem, we must first understand how God's words *ought* to come into the world according to the *Zohar*. It is a process very much like that by which our own words come into the world. The anatomy of divine speech—the cosmic structure that converts God's yearnings into syllables, words, and sentences—is like our own anatomy writ large.

According to the kabbalists, that process starts with Voice, an aspect of divinity that transcends language.[4] The divine Voice, like our vocal chords, emits a call that is deeper than words, that is not yet speech. The call of Voice is like an endless vowel, with no consonant to limit it. It is a stream of longing for connectedness, boundless and undifferentiated. The kabbalists identified Voice with the heart of God. They also gave it the name Truth.

---

3. *Zohar* 2:25b (see Matt edition, vol. 4, 91–92). I am indebted to Melila Hellner-Eshed, who introduced me to this text. For a detailed discussion of the relationship between speech and deeper mystical intuitions in the *Zohar*, see Hellner-Eshed, *River Flows from Eden*, 352–64.

4. Voice (*Kol*), in the *Zohar*, is another name for the divine emanation Splendor (*Tiferet*), which is also called Truth (*Emet*). It is also known by the unpronounceable name YHWH (for which the Jewish tradition generally substitutes the euphemism "Lord"). For the authors of the *Zohar*, the impossibility of pronouncing YHWH was evidence that Voice is above language.

The Exile of Language

In order to become intelligible, the call of Voice must pass through other portals of divinity until it reaches the final one—namely, Articulation. Articulation, like the human mouth, is the interface between God's inner and outer worlds.[5] It is the place where the divine realm meets our own. There, according to the kabbalists, the call of Voice is shaped into syllables, words, and sentences. It is parsed into speech.

But the very parsing that enables us to comprehend Voice limits it as well. The same enunciation that expresses it diminishes it. Articulation makes the endless flow of Voice intelligible, but only by delineating it into segments, making it un-whole. Language, at its best, can speak the truth. But it can never speak the complete truth. Grammar and vocabulary can give form to the infinite, but only by making it finite. They can reveal, but only by obscuring.

God's struggle with language, then, is like our own. Words are necessary and yet insufficient. At the level of Articulation, God attains the power to speak, but only by reducing what is said to what is sayable.

It is by accepting that compromise, according to the *Zohar*, that God—and we—bring words of Torah into the world. At least, that is how it *ought* to happen. But in Egypt, that process broke down. Voice and Articulation became misaligned, each one alienated from the other. The former no longer flowed into the latter. As words and sentences lost touch with Voice, as their stream of meaning dried up, language became trivial and empty. Words rang hollow. They no longer spoke of anything beyond themselves. Speech was trapped in exile.

That was Moses's complaint. As the greatest of the prophets, who most deeply empathized with God, he embodied Voice. But Voice no longer flowed into Articulation.[6] Truth, for lack of access

---

5. Articulation (*Dibbur*), in the *Zohar*, is another name for *Sh'khinah* (Presence) or *Malkhut* (Kingdom), the most immanent emanation of divinity, closest to the human world.

6. The *Zohar* plays on the Hebrew word *milah*, which can mean either

to that final portal, which was now in exile, could no longer make itself known in the world. God's call remained un-parsed, unspoken, because words were empty, voiceless. That Moses could not speak was a symptom of that deeper cosmic discontinuity.

As long as we were still in Egypt, that remained the case. While the Israelites remained in exile, language did as well. Words were just words, cut off from their deeper source of meaning.

But that exile would not last forever. When we reached Mount Sinai, according to the *Zohar*, speech was redeemed. Voice and Articulation came back into alignment. Truth again flowed into sentences and syllables. God spoke from the heart again, and Moses did as well. Words of Torah reentered the world.

II

The problem that the *Zohar* describes—the emptying of language—is probably as old as language itself. We can assume that for as long as human beings have spoken words at all, they have spoken words that were just words. Language, by its very nature, is vulnerable to exile. The inner channel that links heart to mouth, voice to articulation, is a fragile channel. Its flow is a precarious flow which easily dries up. And when that happens, words ring hollow, being cut off from what ought to be their source. Even the words that we entrust to those who are closest to us can degenerate into clichés. Even the words that we say to ourselves, the language of our inner stream of consciousness, can devolve into a tedious litany detached from our true voice.

We send language into exile by many paths. Sometimes, we detach words from their source by allowing them to evaporate into

---

"word" or "circumcision" (since words "cut" the voice into discrete units of meaning and create openings to understanding). In the biblical verse, Moses complains that his lips are uncircumcised, which means, according to the *Zohar*, that he has no words, because his voice has no opening—i.e., no portal of articulation—through which to express itself (*Zohar* 2:25b; Matt 4:91–92).

a haze of self-deception, airy platitudes that lack the capacity to say anything that matters. Fearing silence, we fill the airways with chatter. Or, fearing truth, we puff up language to the point where it no longer has the power to challenge us.

At other times, we send language into exile in the opposite way. Far from making light of words, we rob them of their resonance by making them too heavy. For example, when we fear that we might say the wrong thing, we often compensate by treating words with too much care for their own good. We focus so much on the vessels that we lose sight of their purpose. We forget that words are means, not ends—that the essential thing is the voice.

That is not to mention more malignant ways in which we send words into exile, through deceit and misdirection. The emptying of language as an act of sabotage is also probably as old as words themselves.

So the problem that the *Zohar* spoke of is a perennial one. Human beings have always been guilty of degrading the capacity of language. For varied reasons and by varied means, we have always sinned against speech.

But in our time, the problem has taken on a new dimension. Today, we experience the exile of language not only as a sin but as a condition. At a certain level, we understand the emptiness of language as an intractable fact, a fundamental feature of reality, even apart from our own lapses. We still recognize the *Zohar*'s diagnosis of the problem, but we have less faith in its vision of redemption.

We see that loss of faith perhaps most clearly in the status of religious language. Today, the sacred narratives and metaphors that once charged the world with meaning have lost much of their authority. Modernity has drained the confidence that we once had in their capacity to teach deeper truths. To a growing number of modern ears, those words are just words.

But the problem is broader and deeper than that. It is not only sacred language that has lost much of its force but words in general. Today, we feel an undercurrent of despair about the power of language to capture any truths at all—or, more precisely, a loss of faith that we have any truths that words might capture in the first place. The *Zohar* taught that we could redeem language by speaking from the heart, by realigning our words with our deepest voice. But in this skeptical age, we cannot help but wonder if the heart knows anything at all beyond its own desires and biases—assuming that it knows even those. And if the heart knows nothing deeper than itself, then speaking from the heart solves nothing. Language still lacks traction.

We see evidence of that despair about the power of words in many areas of the contemporary world. We see it, for example, in the decay of political debate. The rhetoric of the reactionary right specifically (where distrust of expertise is greatest) shows an increasing cynicism about what words are for. That rhetoric makes little effort to persuade, to offer a vision of the truth. Instead, it reduces language to a tool to reawaken primal loyalties and stoke grievances.[7] That is a symptom of the broader problem. To the extent that people give up on the hope that political speech might teach, that it might convey principles or knowledge of the world, it degenerates into a tribal cry. It becomes no more than a cudgel or a spur.

We see the same despair in the academic world—ironically, where expertise is *most* valued. For instance, we see it in the field of literary criticism. Instead of reading works of poetry or fiction as attempts to crystallize a vision of the world, or as expressions of aesthetic insights and ideals, many academic critics are content to

---

7. Hannah Arendt documented the ultimate emptying of political speech in her study of the totalitarian regimes of the twentieth century. Nazi and Soviet propagandists wasted little effort making their lies credible, because their purpose was not to convince anyone of their truth. Instead, it was to spread cynicism about words in general. Their goal was not to persuade people to believe them but to dissuade them from believing anything at all, so that they could fill the void with tribalism (Arendt, *Origins of Totalitarianism*, 474).

read those works as nothing more than evidence of social hierarchies. They reduce them to assertions of entitlement by privileged groups, or protests against the same. They assume that there is nothing else of which those works *could* speak—that, in the end, language is about nothing but power. Moreover, they express themselves in opaque terminology that illustrates that very loss of faith in words, jargon cut off from the kind of voice that makes true language live.

Those examples are signs of the time, illustrations of the deeper problem. The state of our political and academic discourse points to the broader loss of trust in language that defines our era. Increasingly, we doubt that language points to anything beyond itself. We understand its exile not as a failure that we have the power to fix but as an irredeemable condition that we must endure.

III

Yet, at a deeper level, we have not lost faith in language altogether. We have not abandoned words entirely to languish in exile. There is a part of us that still implicitly believes that words can be more than just words, that they can capture deeper truths, albeit imperfectly. In an elusive but inescapable way, the *Zohar*'s narrative of the redemption of language still speaks for us.

How does our residual faith in language manifest itself? It reveals itself most vividly in our persistent search for meaning, in our refusal to stop asking fundamental questions, even though the answers might seem unattainable. When we ask ourselves what makes life precious and which principles it ought to point to, we can hear beneath the surface of our struggle a whisper of confidence. In the stubbornness with which we pose those questions, we detect a still, small voice of affirmation, a refusal to give up the hope that language might still *mean*—that it might still say things that ultimately matter. If we were not believers in that sense, we would have silenced our hearts long ago. To state that claim explicitly, to confess that we believe that words might still be able to redeem us if we can redeem them first, is not to take an artificial leap of faith. It is to embrace a faith that is as close to us as our own yearning.

The most persistent forms of faith live not in answers but in questions. We locate them not in particular religious doctrines but in our refusal to stop searching—or perhaps our inability to do so. That applies to what might be the most fundamental faith of all. That is the trust that there are truths deeper than language, and that the human heart has the capacity to glimpse some of those truths and put those glimpses into words, however incompletely.

This suggests a different reading of the *Zohar*'s claim that speaking from the heart can redeem words from exile. Instead of reading it as a naïve teaching, a throwback to a time when truth was less elusive, we can read it as a statement of our own defiance, our refusal to close off our hearts, even today. The text can serve as an expression of the faith that still reveals itself when we look honestly at ourselves, when we examine our own skepticism skeptically. That we persist in seeking something substantive to say, even in the midst of exile, is evidence that we have not lost hope that such a thing is possible, that words can still have meaning, and hence, that life can too.

The Dancer and the Dance

∽

*O body swayed to music, O brightening glance,
How can we know the dancer from the dance?*
WILLIAM BUTLER YEATS[1]

I

If scripture is the work of human beings, how can it command us? If it speaks from within history, expressing the perspectives of a time and place, why should we defer to it?

We often frame the problem of belief in that way, as a matter of the status of our sacred texts. If the voices of the Bible speak from human points of view, how can the text transcend the limits of those points of view? If the Bible's words are human words, why should we grant more weight to them than we would to our own words, or to those of anyone else? The question can be broadened to pertain to those of all faiths who struggle with the challenge of historical perspective. How can one continue to invest authority in any sacred text once its roots in human history have been

---

1. Yeats, "Among School Children," lines 63–64.

exposed? If sacred texts are no more than expressions of their authors' worldviews, products of their time and place, what deference do they deserve?

Having framed the problem of belief in that way, we turn to theology to solve it. Modern Jewish theology in particular has taken that problem deeply to heart. Among the tasks that it has assigned itself—perhaps the main task—is to salvage the authority of the Torah, to preserve its status as a source of truth, through methods that are applicable to all traditions.[2] It strives to rescue the Torah (and, by extension, other sacred texts) from the status of a cultural artifact, once its origins in human history have been revealed.

But theological attempts to solve that problem, in the end, do little more than restate the problem in other terms. Theologians turn to language that seems to square the circle. They argue that the Torah is both human and transcendent, using terms that make room for the subjectivity of the text without surrendering the claim that there is something ultimately true behind it. For instance, they speak of the Torah as a set of "metaphors," as a "response" to revelation rather than revelation itself. They define the Torah as a product of a divine-human encounter, an attempt to capture in the language of a particular culture an absolute that transcends culture, to crystallize in words that which is beyond words. Then, having staked out for the Torah what appears to be a middle ground between the literally factual and the false, they feel that they have preserved for it at least some kind of authority.[3]

---

2. *Torah* (literally, "teaching"), in the narrow sense, refers to the first five books of the Hebrew Bible. In the broad sense, it refers to the entire corpus of Jewish religious teachings, which are rooted in those books.

3. Abraham Joshua Heschel claimed that "as a report about revelation, the Bible itself is a *midrash* [i.e., a human interpretation]" (Heschel, *God in Search*, 185). Louis Jacobs defined the Torah as a "by-product of revelation," as opposed to revelation itself (Jacobs, *Jewish Theology*, 204). Jakob Petuchowski called the biblical narrative of revelation "an echo sounding through the ages of what happened [at Sinai]" (Petuchowski, *Ever Since Sinai*, 67). Neil Gilman

But such solutions just sidestep the problem. To speak of the Torah as a human reading of a transcendent reality solves nothing unless it is *our* reading of that reality—that is, unless we believe it in some sense. After all, metaphors may ring hollow. They may fail to capture anything that we consider true. To refer to the Torah as a set of metaphors (or by some equivalent term) does not spare us from having to ask: Are they metaphors that speak for us, that teach things in which we believe?

So we are back where we started, with the problem of belief. Not only have we failed to solve the problem, but we have failed even to touch on it. The point of intersection that we seek between the relative and absolute remains elusive, like a chimera that we see out of the corner of our eye but that vanishes when we turn to view it head on.

We are back where we started because we started in the wrong place. At its root, the problem is not one of theology but of psychology. Fundamentally, it is not about our texts but about ourselves. The true task before us is not to vindicate particular beliefs but to redeem the possibility of belief itself. The question, in the end, is how we can self-consciously invest our hearts in any claim at all.

The same historical perspective that undermines the absoluteness of the Torah and of other sacred texts eventually undermines the absoluteness of all efforts to make meaning, even our most personal efforts. The same critical detachment that reveals the humanness of every faith tradition, in the end, reveals the humanness of every claim that we might make about what ultimately matters. It renders all truths relative. When we step back far enough, we see that all of our attempts to verbalize what is important in this world are human constructs, products of a time and place, expressions of our subjectivity.

---

defined the Torah as "the classic mythic explanation of one community's experience of the world" (Gillman, *Sacred Fragments*, 31).

So the broader question is this: How can any claim compel us once we have stepped back and recognized the relativity of every truth on which we might attempt to build our lives? Any sentence that begins "I believe . . ."—if the emphasis is on the "I"—seems to collapse into a contradiction. If to believe is to anchor oneself in an absolute, how can I believe in what is merely my belief? How can I subordinate myself to my own subjectivity? To the extent that I own my truths, how can my truths own me?

We cannot think our way out of this trap. Theology will not help us. We can solve it only through a deeper inner evolution. Hence, we follow a different route. Instead of starting with theology, we start with the psychology of the searching self, its struggles and its growth. In the end, we will come back and give theology a more fitting task: not to make belief possible but to express its content, to articulate an outward vision that gives meaning to our inner journey.

II

The talmudic sages, who lived in the early centuries of the Common Era, were untroubled by our question.[4] They experienced the Torah's truth as absolute and relative at the same time, and felt no need to reconcile the tension. Even as they appealed to the text as their ultimate authority, they taught that its meanings hinged on their own subjectivity. Even as they asserted that the Torah spoke from heaven, they insisted that its content was a product of their varied points of view.

In their reflections on their work, the sages claimed the right to innovate, to bring their creativity to bear in their interpretations

---

4. The founders of rabbinic Judaism, called the *hakhamim*, or sages, lived during the first five centuries of the Common Era in Roman Palestine and Sassanian Babylonia. Their literature includes the Mishnah, the Tosefta, the Jerusalem and Babylonian Talmuds, and various collections of midrash, or biblical interpretation.

of the Torah. But they also claimed that even their most radical rereadings of the Torah were intrinsic to the text. They reveled in the humanness of what they taught, but also took it as a given that their teachings were divine. They heard the Torah's teachings as transcendent and, at the same time, as expressions of their own conflicting voices. They taught that two irreconcilable opinions were both "the words of the living God,"[5] that generations of interpretation and reinterpretation representing incompatible beliefs and values had all been given to Moses at Mount Sinai.[6] Without apology—in fact, with pride of authorship—they owned the very teachings that owned them.

And the sages went still further. They projected the two-sidedness of the Torah back to its beginning. That the Torah had the power to command us, even as its meanings were contingent on our points of view, had been the case even at Mount Sinai, before there was a written text at all. Rabbi Yose bar Hanina, for example, taught that all who stood at Sinai heard God's commandments differently. They all received the divine call through the filter of their subjectivity. In other words, even revelation itself had been relative.[7]

To modern ears, the claim that everyone at Sinai, in effect, received a different Torah has anarchic implications. It threatens to nullify the text's authority. We cannot help but ask: If the Torah's meanings are *our* meanings, how can my interpretation of the Torah make a claim on anyone else? If, even at Sinai, every Israelite had his or her own version of the truth, who can say when we are wrong about God's will? And if we cannot be wrong about God's will, why bring God into it at all? Are we not just listening to ourselves?

---

5. BT Eruvin 13b.
6. JT Pe'ah 2:6.
7. Pesikta DRK 12:25.

To us, those questions seem inescapable. But Rabbi Yose bar Hanina and his colleagues felt no need to address them. Why were they so sanguine about questions that seem unavoidable to us? Why were they so unconcerned about defending the authority of the text?

Apparently, it was because they did not recognize the difficulty in the first place. As far as they were concerned, the relativity of the Torah's truths was not a problem to be solved. It was a paradox to be celebrated. That we each have our own Torah was not a threat to the Torah's authority. Instead, it was evidence of the Torah's greatness.

That the sages were so untroubled by a question that claims so much of our intellectual energy points to a difference in their inner makeup. It seems that they did not experience the sharp distinction that we do between what we would call subjective and objective claims. For them, there was no conflict between the Torah's relativity and its absoluteness. That the Torah's meanings were human constructs in no way lessened their authority.

In Jewish history, it was the sages who first, and perhaps most boldly, asserted that paradox. But the underlying psychology was not new with them. Centuries earlier, the authors and redactors of the Bible had apparently experienced their truths in the same mixed way, though they never made the paradox explicit. On the one hand, they made little effort to conceal the human fingerprints that they left on their work. For example, when the editors of Genesis stitched together inconsistent versions of the stories of creation and the patriarchs, they made no attempt to hide the seams, to smooth over the inconsistencies. When the authors of Deuteronomy recast earlier versions of biblical law to bring it into line with their own values, they did not hesitate to draw attention to their sources. They echoed older layers of the Bible, even though their echoes highlight their departures from those very precedents.[8] Biblical wordsmiths felt no need to suppress evidence of their own creativity. But on the other hand, they seem never to have questioned that their work bore the authority of heaven.

What were those biblical authors and redactors thinking as they put the humanness of their work on display? Did they assume, as the sages would centuries later, that conflicting human voices conveyed "the words of the living God,"[9] or that even their most recent reinterpretations of God's word had already been given at Mount Sinai?

We do not know how they would have explained themselves, because they felt so little need to explain. Apparently, they felt no pressure to reconcile the humanness of their work with its divine authority. Having it both ways seems to have presented no problem to them. Perhaps their silence tells us that it was even less an issue for them than it would be for the sages after them. Not only did they feel no need to reconcile the paradox; they felt no need even to note it.

Just as having it both ways did not begin with the sages, it did not end with them either. Their successors—medieval philosophers, mystics, and jurists—were similarly untroubled by their own originality. For them, too, there was no apparent tension between human creativity and heavenly authority. Even as they worked out new interpretations of the Torah, they experienced their work as the recovery of ancient truths, as the articulation of what had always been. They, too, knew no sharp dichotomy between God's truth and their own.

What was it in the inner makeup of premodern teachers of the Torah that enabled them to have it both ways, to innovate without suffering the loneliness of innovation? How could they recreate the Torah in their own image, yet remain unburdened by

---

8. Compare, for example, Deut 15:12–18 with its apparent antecedent, Exod 21:2–7.

9. BT Eruvin 13b.

the responsibility of ownership? How could they own their truths, yet still be owned by them?

To experience our creativity as a problem, to be weighed down by the recognition that even our most precious truths are merely our own, requires a degree of psychological distance that did not exist in the premodern world. Only a self so detached that it can step back and reflect on its own subjectivity from almost every angle can be troubled by the relativity of the truths that it holds most dear. Without that degree of separateness of self, there is no sharp boundary between the personal and the impersonal. The distinction that we take as fundamental between truths that we construct and those that are larger than ourselves is much less clear. There is nothing more natural in that state than having it both ways.

In other words, what freed premodern teachers of the Torah to innovate as they did was their lack of distance from the past. The tightness of the bond between the generations in their world left no room for the critical self that we know to emerge. It did not allow for self-awareness as we experience it, which is born of inner dislocation from the past. They were free to reshape the tradition in their own image because they had so little sense of themselves as distinct from that tradition. They did not know the dancer from the dance.

From where we stand, that absence of self-consciousness might seem naïve. The blurring together of self and nonself, the lack of what we think of as a clearly delineated *I*, is a trait that we ascribe to the mind of a child.[10] But if we are tempted to look with condescension at those who came before us, that tells us only that modern culture, like most cultures, holds up its own psychological traits as the standard for others to meet. If, however, we use our

---

10. Consider, for example, James Fowler's model of faith development, which is premised on a modern understanding of psychological maturity. I would argue that even the most sophisticated premodern thinkers would have risen no higher than stage 3 on Fowler's scale of 6 (see Fowler, *Stages of Faith*).

self-awareness to its full advantage, it enables us *not* to condescend. Our recognition of the *I* behind our judgments leads us to a healthy humility, an acknowledgment that our way of defining a mature self is not the only way.

III

The intellectual revolutions of the postmedieval world were all expressions of a new degree of psychological separateness, a new creative alienation. The rise of the experimental method in the natural sciences, based on critical observation and inquiry as opposed to deference to authority, was one example. Another was the rise of critical history, which exposed the cultural underpinnings of sacred traditions. A third was the new preoccupation with epistemology in early modern philosophy. Epistemology begins with this question: How can we know anything beyond our own minds? But only a self that is no longer subsumed by tradition and community, one newly conscious of the loneliness out of which it views the world, would feel the need to ask that question in the first place.

The rise of individualism in the political and social spheres, the shift from the medieval world of interlocking obligations to the modern world of individual rights and liberties, expressed the same internal evolution. To create—or even to conceive of—a community that revolved around the individual required a new kind of self, one capable of bearing the burden of autonomy.

Given the weight that modern culture places on the individual, it is no wonder that it takes so long to grow up in our world. When growing up meant stepping into predetermined roles, adolescence barely existed. But modern culture, which defines becoming an adult as choosing who we are to be, invented what it could not do without: an extended period of time between childhood and adulthood in which to struggle with the turmoil of individuation.

It invented psychotherapy as well, and for the same reason. In its various forms, psychotherapy is about emotional separation. By stepping back and gaining new perspective on the conflicts that we struggle with, the patterns that we reenact, we enable ourselves to make choices about them rather than be controlled by them. Through self-awareness, we increase our freedom. We come to function as individuals rather than as extensions of our family history. Then, having achieved that distance and perspective, we reconnect with family from a new, less conflictual position. The new bond is different from the childhood bond. Now, it is the self that defines the relationship as much as the relationship defines the self.

Modernity, then, is about the emergence of a self that is exhilaratingly free but painfully aware of the aloneness out of which it views the world, capable of extraordinary independence but deeply conscious of its subjectivity. In other words, it is about no longer being able to have it both ways. Having stepped back and seen ourselves and those who came before us from a distance, we live with the relativity of our truths.

Or we make a different choice. We reject the distance that modernity gave us in an effort to return to what we once had, to trade self-consciousness for certainty. We take refuge in reactionary forms of faith, which struggle to uphold authority by suppressing separateness. We hear God's voice again by silencing our own.

But ironically, with that attempt to turn back time, we find ourselves not back where we once were but somewhere else entirely. A faith that fears critical distance is not the same as one that never knew it in the first place.[11] Unlike premodern faith, it sustains authority at the cost of spontaneity and flexibility. It enforces solidarity by adding stringencies on top of stringencies. It defends the timelessness of its truths by suppressing creativity in the

---

11. See Paul Tillich's distinction between "natural literalism" and "reactive literalism" (Tillich, *Dynamics of Faith*, 52).

present and denying that we ever had it in the past. And so, we find that in return for half the prize, we have given up the other half.

That is the toll of modernity: that we must choose. We can celebrate the liberated self that modernity created, or we can suppress it. But we cannot live in innocence of it.

> A parable: To what can it be compared? To a circle of dancers. Their hands interlocked, they dance with an effortless grace as natural as their breathing. Their steps subtly change, their choreography unfolds, but they do not stumble. The dance seems to flow through them. They have no awareness of their separateness from it. The dancers and the dance are one.
>
> Then, at one moment, they look down at their moving feet and recognize that the steps are their steps, that the dance is their dance, that they are distinct from it. And with that awareness, they begin to stumble, first a few of them, then most of them. Their dancing becomes labored and deliberate. They fall back from the circle and stop.
>
> But some of them do not stop. Instead, they lock arms and dance even faster than they did before, so that they will not dare to look down at their feet. The dance, for them, becomes more forced and strenuous, because only by increasing its intensity and rigor can they keep themselves from looking down, recognizing that the steps are theirs, and stumbling.

So it is with us. Having distinguished between the dancer and the dance, we can live with that self-consciousness and pay the price in meaning, or we can suppress our self-awareness. But we cannot go back to what we had before. The natural integrity that we once had is gone.

Still, there is a third response to the disruption of the dance which points beyond the limits of the parable. Instead of giving in to our paralysis or struggling to turn back time, we can choose a new path forward which will renew the possibility of faith. We can seek a new integrity of past and present, a healing of the rift between the two. The breaking of the vessels cannot be undone—nor would we wish it to be undone. But we can seek a new cement with which to mend them, which will be as strong as the original clay. We can search for a new way to commit ourselves without surrendering ourselves, to dance in the full light of self-awareness.

IV

In 1920 in Frankfurt am Main, Franz Rosenzweig envisioned a new kind of Jewish learning which pointed toward that new integrity. Addressing Jewish seekers of his time, whom modernity had uprooted from the past, he mapped out a new intellectual and spiritual path. He called on his listeners to reclaim the texts of their tradition without surrendering their distance, to make their way from detachment to engagement, while bringing their perspective as outsiders with them.

> A new learning is about to be born—rather, it has been born ... It is a learning in reverse order. A learning that no longer starts from the Torah and leads into life, but the other way round: from life, from a world that knows nothing of the Law, or pretends to know nothing, back to the Torah. That is the sign of the time. It is the sign of the time because it is the mark of the men of the time. There is no one today who is not alienated, or who does not contain within himself some small fraction of alienation ... We all know that in being Jews we must not give up anything, not renounce anything, but lead everything back to Judaism. From the periphery back to the center; from the outside, in.[12]

The goal of this new learning, as Rosenzweig envisioned it, would be a synthesis of faith and critical self-consciousness. His claim was not just that the two apparent opposites could live together but that the latter could and ought to be the engine of the former. We could use our intellectual distance to reclaim the past

---

12. Rosenzweig, "On Jewish Learning," 231.

and make it our own. We could use our inner liberty to ground our lives in something larger than liberty itself.

The kind of faith that Rosenzweig proposed would be unlike premodern faith. It would differ not only in its content but in its emotional dimensions. Premodern faith had little room within it for an emotionally distinct, self-conscious *I*. This new kind of faith would be accessible only to such an *I*. Ancient and medieval faith excluded anything like modern autonomy. This new faith would require it.

But, in one respect at least, the faith that Rosenzweig proposed would be like the faith that we had lost. To bring our alienation with us from the outside in would mean to have it both ways once again. It would mean to own our faith and yet be owned by it, to consciously write our own Torah and yet be commanded by it nonetheless. In that sense, it would mean recovering what our ancient and medieval ancestors had, albeit in a new way.

How do we reach that destination? Or, more fundamentally, is there really such a place at all, where distance comes full circle to engagement, where we stand outside and inside at the same time?

As we have seen, we cannot merely think our way to such a place. If we conceive of Rosenzweig's journey strictly as an intellectual one, a matter of the mind, then his vision contradicts itself. His promise is no more than a restatement of the problem. To be outside is, by definition, *not* to be inside. But if we understand the journey not as a matter of the mind alone but as a deeper evolution of the self, then we can see how we might move beyond that contradiction after all.

What is the path that that deeper journey would have to take, beneath the surface of our efforts to reclaim the text? In which direction, at that deeper level, would we have to move? Our direction would have to be *outward*, not inward. It would have to be toward greater independence, not greater deference. For most of those who grew up with at least a residual loyalty to a religious tradition, reclaiming sacred content requires a simultaneous movement *away* from the voices of the text to a place where the gravitational pull of the past is weaker. To make the past our own again, we must venture further afield.

Why? Because the psychological detachment that typifies modernity is *merely* critical. Modern culture makes us free, but not as free as we imagine. What we have spoken of thus far as paralyzing self-awareness—crippling detachment from the past—is, at a deeper level, awkward in-betweenness. That we experience our freedom as corrosive to the possibility of meaning indicates that we have stepped back only so far. That our self-consciousness feels incompatible with belief in anything at all means that we are stuck in a halfway position, neither here nor there. In that sense, it is our *lack* of distance that excludes us from the dance. Before we can reclaim the past on our own terms, we need more room to do so.

What does it mean to venture further outward? It means to detach ourselves from our detachment, to see our distance from a distance, and in the process come to recognize that we are not as independent as we thought we were. It means to reflect on ourselves from a point of view so separate that we see that separateness itself is never absolute.

Critical detachment is lonely, but not as lonely as we imagine. After all, the spiritual paralysis that we have been describing is a *cultural* phenomenon. Like every spiritual crisis, it arises out of shared assumptions—in this case, those of late modern individualism. If our paralysis feels intractable, it is because the premises behind it seem so basic that we do not question them. In that respect, our alienation is itself a matter of allegiance to convention. Our uprootedness is evidence of rootedness in a particular time and place. When we step back and view the problem of belief from a still more detached perspective, it appears not as a symptom of ultimate aloneness but as an expression of a kind of solidarity, of loyalty to the assumptions of our culture.

The Dancer and the Dance

As human beings, we are defined by our allegiances, whether we know it or not. Our interpretations of reality are always shaped by our attachments. To reach the distance where we see that that is still true, even of our critical selves, brings us to a different diagnosis of the problem. From that greater distance, we see that it is not distance per se that is the source of our paralysis but the opposite: our attachment to an unexamined article of faith. If self-consciousness cuts off our path to meaning, it is because we are not being self-conscious enough. We are granting unearned absoluteness to the critical point of view.

How does the world look once we have stretched ourselves still further, once we have reached a point of view beyond the merely critical, where detachment is detached even from itself? Perhaps the first to speak of what he saw from that position was William James. In 1896, a generation before Rosenzweig, he pointed out the logical fallacy of privileging the critical perspective. In response to the rigid scientific skeptics of his time who dismissed religious claims because they were unprovable, James pointed out that they were guilty of the very thing that they deplored. They were doing exactly what they claimed not to be doing—namely, deferring to a dogma. In a case where to believe or not believe is a binary choice, where both are plausible options and where there will never be proof one way or the other, to declare that disbelief is the only valid choice is to put one's finger on the scale based on nothing but pure faith.

> When I look at the religious question, as it really puts itself to concrete men . . . then this command that we shall put a stopper on our hearts, instincts, and courage, and *wait*—acting of course meanwhile more or less as if religion were *not* true—till doomsday, or till such time as our intellect and senses working together may have raked in evidence enough,—this command, I say, seems to me the queerest idol ever manufactured in the philosophic cave . . . . If we are empiricists, if we believe that

> no bell in us tolls to let us know for certain when truth is in our grasp, then it seems a piece of idle fantasticality to preach so solemnly our duty of waiting for the bell.[13]

James spoke as a philosopher, but he was modeling a cognitive shift that takes place at a level deeper than the intellect alone. To internalize his argument requires a repositioning of the whole self. To see the world as he proposes is to step back so far that we come to recognize that detachment itself is a form of connectedness, that there is no escape from faith. It is to stand at such a distance that we realize that no matter where we stand, we see reality refracted through the prism of what James called "passions,"[14] but which we could also call *loyalties*. There is no place free of cultural and social gravity.

To be clear, this outlook where detachment looks back at itself is very different from the rigid relativism that we often call postmodern. The latter makes it a principle to undermine all principles and adopts as its core value the deflation of all values. It fervently believes in deconstructing all beliefs, reducing all ideals to the defense of power and privilege. In that respect, it is a surrender to spiritual paralysis, not an answer to it. Instead of renewing our capacity to affirm, it celebrates cynicism. Instead of redeeming us from the crippling in-betweenness where we find ourselves, it makes a virtue of that in-betweenness.

The perspective that I am describing requires a step beyond that in-between position. It demands still more distance. To reach it, we must step back so far that we see that even rigid relativism is itself relative, that even the insistence on reducing principles to cultural constructs is itself obedience to a cultural construct. To privilege negation over affirmation, to assume uncritically that undermining meaning is more honest than affirming it, is itself an act of faith.

---

13. James, "Will to Believe," 60–61.
14. James, "Will to Believe," 50.

When we reach that greater distance, when we realize that the thin air of negation has no special purity, we gain the power to affirm again. At that point, there is no longer any contradiction between faith and self-awareness. We no longer experience them as mutually exclusive. Not only *can* we watch ourselves believing, but we cannot help but do so. To observe ourselves at all is to observe ourselves—even our most critical selves—allied with other voices, past and present.

Hence, not only can we choose what to believe, but we *must* do so. The question that we have struggled with thus far—How can I believe self-consciously?—falls away. The question now becomes this: *What*—or, more precisely, *where*—shall I believe self-consciously? In which tradition and community shall I choose to root myself as I struggle to make meaning? Which spiritual language shall I speak as I attempt to make sense of the world and my place in it? Radical self-consciousness resolves the problem that self-consciousness created in the first place. It makes it possible to stand outside and inside at the same time. In fact, it makes it impossible not to do so. In that way, it fuels the new kind of religious searching that Rosenzweig prescribed.

The faith that we arrive at with this new degree of distance is not threatened by the knowledge that there are other options. Its seriousness is not compromised by the awareness of the *I* that has chosen it and must continually choose it anew. It has no need to defend itself against detached critique, because it never relied on the suppression of detachment in the first place. Having nothing to prove, it does not fear moderation. The capacity for conscious choice is now the engine of its own transcendence.

V

What is the substance of a Jewish faith with this new degree of freedom at its core? What kind of religious vision emerges out of a self-conscious reengagement with the past? What is the form of the new dance?

With that question, we shift back from psychology to theology, from process to content. We return to where we started. But we do so with a difference. Now, we do not ask theology to make meaning possible, to solve the problem of belief. Instead, we assign it a more modest task: to give shape to our faith. We turn to it in search of language to express our vision from this new position, to put our new commitment into words.

The *what* of our belief need not, by any logical necessity, be a reflection of the *how*. But if we seek a unity of self, we will need there to be harmony between the two. We will naturally turn to a theology that mirrors our psychology, that takes into account the inner process by which we have arrived at it and by which we sustain it. We will seek a faith whose lyrics fit its underlying music.

Such a theology would be one of separation and reintegration, of moving outward for the sake of moving inward. It would be a narrative of shattering the idols for the sake of hearing God's call, of venturing into the desert as a path to Sinai.

It would also be a theology of pluralism, a narrative that validates respect for differences and mirrors the internal openness that comes with having made real choices, with knowing that we could have chosen differently, that our way is not the only way.

There could be many such narratives. What follows is my own:

> In the beginning, God was everything and therefore nothing, because there is no definition, no identity, without relationship. "You are my witnesses, says the Lord, and I am God."[15] Rabbi Shimon bar Yohai interpreted that to mean "If you are my witnesses, says the Lord, then I am God, and if you are not my witnesses, then it is as if I am not God."[16]

---

15. Isa 43:12.
16. Pesikta DRK 12:6.

The Dancer and the Dance

The creation of the world, then, was at the same time God's self-creation. It came out of God's will to love, and hence to be.

To create, God had to make room for the other. Therefore, creation began with a divine contraction.[17] That original separation is the source of our existence and of God's existence in relation to us. There could be no world had God not stepped back.

The darkness of this world is the result of that divine separation. It is God's tragedy, and ours, that to exist—to have the separateness that makes connection possible—is to know brokenness. It is the price that we, and God, pay for the opportunity to love. And it is through love that we redeem that brokenness.

To be an image of God is to empathize with God's need for connectedness, to crave self-definition and the sense of meaning that comes with it. It is the essence of our humanness.

But often, we forget the source of that need, its origin in empathy with the divine. Unaware of the true nature of our need, we express it in distorted and destructive ways. We define ourselves through competition and exploitation, through dehumanizing ideologies and xenophobic hatreds. We find meaning in corrosive forms of connectedness which cut us off from our own humanness and that of others.

That is idolatry—our embrace of values that obscure the image of God in us and in each other. To remember who we really are, we must step back and shatter those idols in a new act of radical separation. In the letting go of what we think we know, the separation that makes room for true relationship, we reenact God's original separation for the sake of love.

At those moments, when we liberate ourselves from our enslavement and venture out into the desert, we arrive at Sinai. We realize that our need for meaning, for connectedness, is part of a larger need. Our empathy with God becomes a conscious empathy. We feel called upon to act on God's behalf. We feel called upon to love. Those moments are moments of revelation—or, more precisely, of God's self-revelation. "Humanity is

---

17. *Tzimtzum* in the terminology of Lurianic kabbalah. See Scholem, *Major Trends*, 260–61.

precious, being images of God—more precious still in that it has been made known to them that they are images of God."[18]

Through that conscious, active empathy, we add to creation what God could not create alone: our reciprocity. In imitating God, we complete the other half of the relationship and, in that way, bring God more fully into existence. In that way, we contribute to redemption.

Just as often, or perhaps more often, instead of revelation leading to redemption, the reverse occurs. When we act with true compassion in the world, we sense that our love is part of a greater love. By placing ourselves in alignment with God, we open ourselves to revelation. "You shall love your neighbor as yourself; I am the Lord."[19]

Communities that are rooted in respect for humanness develop patterns of sacred practice as a tree sprouts leaves. Those ways of worshiping and working in the world are the means by which such communities remind themselves, and teach others, that all human beings are created in God's image. Other cultures have their sacred patterns, which they call by other names. We honor theirs, even as we cherish our own. "The righteous of all nations have a share in redemption."[20]

The experience that we have spoken of in the language of psychology—the separation and reintegration of the self—is the same experience that we now speak of in the language of theology. But neither language can replace the other. They interpret that experience from different cognitive positions.

From the outside, in the language of radical self-consciousness, we speak of claiming our right to believe, of giving ourselves freedom to choose. From the inside, in the language of the

---

18. M Avot 3:18.

19. Lev 19:18. Martin Buber understood the second half of the verse, "I am the Lord [YHWH]," to be a consequence of the first half, "You shall love your neighbor as yourself." In other words, we experience the divine through love of neighbor (Buber, "Silent Question," 212).

20. MT Teshuvah 3:5.

believing self, we speak of shattering the idols, of making ourselves as ownerless as the desert so that we can receive the Torah anew.[21]

Our integrity depends on our remaining true to our bilingualism. It is the richness of our lives to speak from both positions, to bring our self-awareness with us to the center of our faith, to know the dancer from the dance, and yet to dance.

---

21. Num. Rabbah 1:7.

The New Middle Ground

∼

I

For much of the twentieth century, American Judaism was concentrated at its center. Its dominant religious movement (in which I served as a rabbi in the early years of my career) was Conservative Judaism, a movement known for its blend of traditionalism and liberalism. The movement's intellectual leaders balanced reverence for sacred texts with scholarly skepticism. Its synagogues combined respect for ancient ritual forms with openness to innovation. To be sure, the movement never truly closed the gap between the two sides of itself. It was more a compromise than a true synthesis. But in taking both sides seriously, it held the center.

Conservative Judaism still claims what remains of that center. But the movement has been in decline for decades due to the contraction of that middle ground. Traditionalist and liberal Judaism have grown more polarized today, which makes compromise more difficult. Increasingly, the Jewish world, like the religious world in general, is torn between unbridgeable extremes.

The New Middle Ground

Why has the center not held? Why has the middle ground that dominated American Judaism for decades grown so tenuous? Most often, we explain the process demographically, as an effect of ethnic assimilation. The centrist Jews who populated Conservative synagogues at their peak, during the postwar era, were viscerally traditional in their hearts and liberal in their heads. As the children and grandchildren of immigrants, they felt a need to balance their loyalty to the Jewish past with their commitment to the American future. Conservative Judaism represented a comfortable, if not always consistent, equilibrium between those poles. It expressed their ethnic solidarity as well as their determination to be full participants in an open society. In that way, it offered them a natural home.

More recently, the weakening of ethnic loyalty among liberal American Jews has loosened the glue that bound them to tradition. Those born since the second half of the twentieth century share their parents' openness to the secular world, but without the tribal allegiance that once moderated it. Because their liberalism is no longer balanced and restrained by that allegiance, moderate traditionalism is no longer their default position. Hence, the center has eroded.

That narrative is true as far as it goes, but it is too narrow to tell the whole story. If we widen the frame, we see that the erosion of the center is due not only to our integration into the American mainstream but also to changes within the mainstream itself. Religious centrism has declined not only in the Jewish world but in the West in general. To fully understand the hollowing out of the middle, we have to look beyond our own story and examine the broader evolution of modern faith, in particular liberal faith.

II

First of all, what is liberal faith? We can define it, paradoxically, as faith in doubt, the sanctification of skepticism. The term refers to strands of Christianity and Judaism that embraced individual liberty—in particular, the liberty to think for oneself—as a religious value in the nineteenth and twentieth centuries. Liberal faith taught that the modern mind, freed from the shackles of the past, could be a messianic force—that its twin offspring, science and democracy, could redeem the world. It gave its blessing to the modern confidence in technological and social progress, and framed that confidence in the language of the Bible.

We Jews embraced that faith with a unique enthusiasm. Having suffered more than most under the medieval order, and having been invited late to the table of modernity, we came to the table with a special hunger. For us, the liberation of the individual had a practical urgency. It meant redemption from the ghetto and the promise of full citizenship in the modern world. Hence, liberalism has been an essential feature of most modern forms of Judaism, from the left through the broad center. In the twentieth century, it played a key role in Conservative Judaism's modernizing mission to the children and grandchildren of Eastern European immigrants.

But in recent decades, liberal faith has undergone a change that saps much of its spiritual power and makes it harder to square with traditional allegiances of any kind. Its commitment to autonomy has grown more radical and absolutist, to the point that it is hard-pressed to sustain community at all. The old middle ground has fallen away because the two poles that once lived side by side within it can no longer coexist. Liberalism and traditionalism are intrinsically more polarized today than they once were.

As we have noted, Conservative Judaism thrived in the twentieth century because it reflected the ambivalence of partially acculturated American Jews. Its mixture of liberalism and traditionalism, though not entirely consistent, met an urgent need for Jews of that era. Conservative Judaism was able to meet that need because religious liberalism at that time was still compatible to some extent with deep allegiance to the past. Liberalism and traditionalism, though in tension with each other, could still inhabit the same mind.

Liberal faith at that time still had much in common with traditional faith. It made demands on the individual. It offered a vision of redemption, albeit a human-centered rather than a God-centered one. Like all rebellions against the past, it borrowed heavily from that which it rebelled against. It honored biblical categories, even as it reinterpreted them.

To put it in a different way, liberalism and traditionalism at least agreed about what they were fighting over. The disputes between them were like the disputes that religious movements had always had with one another, disagreements over how to answer questions that they shared: What are we to live for? What is ultimately true and important? For all their differences, they agreed on what religion is supposed to do—namely, ground the individual in larger principles and commitments.

Hence, it still made sense to try to harmonize them. Theoreticians of Conservative Judaism who sought to reconcile its two poles had their work cut out for them, to be sure. And I would argue that they never truly succeeded. But the task at least seemed plausible.[1]

But today, the gap between liberal and traditionalist faith is so wide that we can no longer imagine harmonizing them. Liberal faith has evolved to a new stage, at which it no longer functions as faith in the normal sense at all. It has largely given up asking

---

1. Mordecai Kaplan's Reconstuctionism (originally a school of thought within Conservative Judaism) was an example of such a harmonizing project. In offering a liberal rationale for traditional observance, Kaplan meant to bring the old into line with the new, in much the same way that religious thinkers had in earlier centuries.

ultimate questions, let alone answering them. Instead of sanctifying human freedom as a means to higher ends, it now largely treats autonomy as an end in itself.

That traps liberalism in a contradiction. Faith, by definition, orients the individual by something larger than the self. It grounds the self in a greater source of meaning. If faith is faith, it cannot merely be about our own prerogatives. Just as words that are entirely self-referential have no meaning, faith that is entirely about the self points nowhere.

To be sure, liberalism still has *moral* force today. It can still inspire people to push back against injustices and bigotries in the name of individual dignity. In an era of reactionary backlash, that is something to be grateful for. But as a *spiritual* force, a source of ultimate meaning, it no longer meets the need that it once did. To orient us in the universe, to teach us why we are alive, it is not enough to fight for individual freedom as a value in its own right. We must invest that freedom with significance beyond itself. We must frame it in transcendent terms. No longer having the vocabulary to do so, liberal faith has fallen back to a defensive posture. It still resists the subjugation of the self, but it is hard-pressed to say why freedom ultimately matters.

How did liberalism lose its spiritual power, its sense of greater meaning? Some say that it was due to the catastrophes of the twentieth century and the disillusionment that they engendered. Eugene Borowitz has argued that the God who failed at Auschwitz was not the God of Moses but the God of the Enlightenment.[2] Human progress, born of free thinking, gave rise in the end to mechanized brutality in two world wars. It proved to be a false messiah.

That is true as far as it goes, but it misses a deeper point. Even if the wars of the twentieth century had never occurred, liberal faith was still bound to decline. Its own internal logic made that unavoidable. Faith in skepticism will ultimately grow skeptical

---

2. Borowitz, *Renewing the Covenant*, 41.

even of itself. An ethic of critical questioning, in the end, will question even its own motivating principles. As the liberal mind evolved, as it grew more detached from its traditional roots, it was inevitable that it would someday cut itself off from its supply of spiritual fuel. It was destined to reach a point where it had no principle left except the right to be free of coercion.

One symptom of the hollowing out of liberal faith is the spiritual consumerism that has become the organizing principle of most liberal synagogues today, regardless of denomination. Lacking a language of ultimate meaning, they fall back on the subjectivism of the marketplace, in which the customer is always right. Implicitly—and sometimes explicitly—they define their members as their customers, their services and programs as their product, and the satisfaction of their members' spiritual needs as their religious mission.

But the effect of that redefinition is to leave their members spiritually adrift. To be sure, the best liberal synagogues still make ethical demands. But for lack of any larger narrative of sacred obligation, they have no way to contextualize those demands, to say what they ultimately mean. The result is that they struggle to articulate a spiritual mandate larger than the satisfaction of subjective tastes and preferences.

Hence, they doom themselves to disappoint. Meaning, as we have seen, requires an external reference point, a mandate larger than the self. If I have no magnetic north beyond myself, my inner compass will point nowhere in particular. Yet, as self-defeating as the language of spiritual consumerism is, it is the only language of religious mission that liberal faith has left. Its internal evolution leaves it with no other way to speak. It has been emptied out by its own logic.

The spiritual collapse of liberal faith has opened the door to a fierce backlash. Reactionary critics of modernity seize on liberalism's weakness to advance their attack. They point to its crisis as evidence that the Enlightenment was a mistake from the beginning. They insist that only by suppressing modern individualism altogether can we live with meaning again.

In the process, they distort the very past that they claim to defend. In their anti-humanistic zeal, they drain traditional faith of its native creativity and render it rigid and defensive. They transform the past into something that it never was, a hard-edged weapon for our modern culture wars. In that way, they widen the divide from the other side.

Now we can more fully answer the question that we started with: Why has the old center not held? It is because the liberalism of the head and the traditionalism of the heart that once made up that center are now too polarized to coexist. The two halves of the old ambivalence, which once lived in creative equilibrium, have broken apart. Visceral allegiance to tradition still exists among liberal Jews, particularly in the older generation. But it is harder to square with what religious liberalism has become.

In other words, the decline of the old center is due not only to the particulars of our demography but to the state of modern faith in general. Not only are there fewer people seeking the old compromise, but the compromise itself is less available. Moderate traditionalists of the old school who might wish to balance the two sides of themselves face a more difficult challenge today. By that I mean not just an intellectual challenge but a deeper psychological one. At the most fundamental level, the old center has declined because the emotional ground on which it stood, where autonomy and allegiance overlapped, has fallen away.

III

But even as the old middle ground declines, a new but very different middle ground is taking its place. In the Jewish world, it can be found in mainstream synagogues, where it challenges the

The New Middle Ground

prevailing culture of spiritual consumerism, serving as a force for renewal. But it tends to be most concentrated in alternative spiritual communities, which consciously attempt to move beyond the liberal dead end.[3] Sidney Schwarz has called them "covenantal communities," in contrast with the "synagogue centers" that still organize themselves around the liberal paradigm.[4]

The character of this new spiritual centrism is familiar by now. Yet it still seems paradoxical when viewed through a conventional lens. Its sensibility is deeply serious yet nonauthoritarian, reverent yet capable of distance and irony. It honors traditional forms without suppressing spontaneity. It is comfortable with metaphor, but not so comfortable that it forgets that it is metaphor. It feels little need to rationalize faith and rarely turns to apologetics, but it is deeply rational in its respect for science and history. Unlike contemporary liberalism, it does not make an idol of autonomy. But unlike most forms of orthodoxy, it does not suppress autonomy either. It does not hesitate to speak the language of commandedness and obligation, but it takes it as a given that we speak that language by choice.

Arthur Green and others have called this new religious sensibility "postmodern."[5] But it is very different from the rigid relativism that goes by the same name. In a sense, it is the opposite. Postmodernism in the latter sense makes a virtue of negating. It undermines all principles and ideals by reducing them to the defense of power and privilege. It insists that there are no truths, only vested interests. But this new sensibility renews the

---

3. In the American Jewish world, the first of these new communities was Havurat Shalom in Somerville, Massachusetts (which, for a few years in the early 1980s, was my spiritual home). Havurat Shalom was founded in 1968 by Arthur Green and his associates as part of a rebellion against mainstream postwar Judaism. In the decades since, it has inspired a host of new Jewish spiritual communities, directly and indirectly.

4. Schwarz, "Covenantal Community."

5. Green, *Radical Judaism*, 9–13.

possibility of affirmation. Instead of deconstructing principles, it reconstructs them. Instead of undermining ideals, it invests them with new energy. One might argue that it is more deserving of the name postmodern in that it is more truly *post*.[6] It is not content to make its home amid the ruins of liberal faith, where a sense of ultimate purpose is no longer possible. Instead, it moves beyond those ruins.

The new middle ground is not an intellectual position in the narrow sense. To be sure, it tends to favor certain kinds of ideas over others, but it is not fundamentally a matter of ideas. It is fluid in its theology because it is not purely a function of thinking. The journey that brings one to this new vantage point is a psychological journey, a repositioning of the whole self. Substantively, that process can express itself in any number of ways.

In part due to its lack of a fixed ideology, the new middle ground may seem more a patchwork than an integrated position. But, in fact, it has a deeper integrity than the old one did. It is not an expression of ambivalence, which cries out for harmonization. Instead, it manifests a deeper synthesis.

IV

How does this new sensibility escape the dead end that contemporary liberal faith has reached without renouncing liberalism's accomplishments? How does it locate authority beyond the individual without surrendering the right to think for oneself?

To answer that question, we must start by reconceptualizing the collapse of liberal faith. What appears to be its end point, its

---

6. For an example of postmodernism that is not really *post*, consider Stanley Fish. He deconstructs liberal principles, insisting that they are not principles at all but expressions of vested interests. In doing so, he implicitly claims a high ground for his skeptical point of view. But his privileging of negation over affirmation—of critical detachment over principled engagement—is itself a residue of modernism (see Fish, *Trouble with Principle*).

reductio ad absurdum, is better understood as an untenable midpoint in its evolution. The problem with contemporary liberal faith is not that it has grown too radical but that it still is not radical enough. It has collapsed into subjectivism because it is stuck in a halfway position, like a transmission that cannot engage.

To be sure, the liberation of the modern mind from the authority of the past eventually degenerates into corrosive skepticism, which undermines the very faith that justified that liberation in the first place. At a certain point in its development, liberal faith consumes itself. But the subjectivism that is left, which recognizes no authority except the self, is still not as skeptical as it might be.

I have suggested that spiritual consumerism is what remains of liberal faith once it has ceased to be a faith. But that is not exactly right. In fact, liberal faith, even in its hollowed-out form, still rests on a creed, albeit an implicit one. That creed is that, however short on substance it might be, subjectivism at least reckons with religious doubt and therefore stands for intellectual integrity. However problematic it might be to make the self the center of our universe, at least it is more honest than the alternatives. The remnant of liberal faith is still a faith in that it trusts in that last truth.

But when we step back to a still-greater distance and examine that last tacit article of faith, it, too, collapses. From a still more skeptical position, we see that that defense of spiritual consumerism is as vulnerable to doubt as any other faith claim. A value system that revolves around the self and its prerogatives is no less a subjective construct than one that revolves around any other seeming absolute. To make a principle of satisfying personal preferences is in itself a personal preference. It, too, rests on nothing more than a cultural convention, albeit a uniquely modern one.

What remains, then, once the liberated mind has undermined the absoluteness even of its last fallback position? What is left once we have recognized that even the most empty subjectivism is itself subjective?

At that point, our logic abruptly shifts. We cannot help but ask: If retrenching to subjectivism has gained us nothing in intellectual integrity and cost us so much in meaning, what is the point of staying there? If there is no refuge from believing, since any stand or anti-stand that we might take must come down to a matter of belief, why not make a virtue of necessity and claim the right to say what we authentically believe?

There is a kind of leap of faith that is a leap of language. It is a decision, not to submit to the authority of other voices, but to liberate our own, to embrace a language with the power to unlock convictions that we otherwise would have no means to access or express. It is true that we can never rise entirely above cultural constructs. To speak at all is to defer to a vocabulary, a set of paradigms and symbols rooted in the past. But that recognition is the very thing that liberates us to decide which language we will speak. Having come to see that we have no choice but to anchor ourselves somewhere, we are free to anchor ourselves in a spiritual tradition with the richness and the resonance to give voice to our deepest intuitions—in particular, our intuition that there is something larger than ourselves to worship. Paradoxically, the knowledge that there is no escape from the weight of culture and community liberates us to speak from the heart.

In that way, radical skepticism comes full circle and enables us to affirm. It renews our capacity to commit. The kind of faith that we arrive at in this way has a naïveté to it. Unlike liberal faith, it looks out at the world from something like our natural vantage point, a position of allegiance to tradition. But it is not the same as simple, precritical faith, which knew no other point of view. It is naiveté that knows that it is naiveté and also knows that there is no alternative.[7] In that sense, it is faith with skepticism at its heart.

---

7. Compare Paul Ricoeur's concept of a "second naïveté" (Ricoeur, *Symbolism of Evil*, 351).

The New Middle Ground

That is the kind of faith that lives at the new middle ground. The varieties of Judaism whose traits we described above, which stand within tradition and outside it at the same time, come naturally to one who has emerged on the far side of skepticism. The moderation that we find at the new center is not of the old type, which consisted of a compromise between competing poles. Now, there is no longer any tension between faith and intellectual distance, heart and head. For one whose faith is born of skepticism, there is no need to split the difference. The two are one.

The new middle ground is bound to be smaller than the old one was. Conservative Judaism was the dominant American Jewish movement for much of the twentieth century because it offered a default home for partially acculturated Jews. The new middle ground, on the other hand, is not a default position but an intentional one. One does not gravitate to it but chooses it.

Nevertheless, for those who will not trade away their intellectual freedom in return for meaning, nor live with a divided self, there is no other choice. The new middle ground is their only true home.

The Divine "I-Will-Be"

~

Moses said to God, "When I come to the Israelites and say to them 'The God of your ancestors has sent me to you,' and they ask me 'What is His name?' what shall I say to them?" God said to Moses, "I will be what I will be."[1] [God then] said, "Thus shall you say to the Israelites: 'I-Will-Be has sent me to you.'"[2]

I

As he receives his mission at the burning bush, Moses wants to know who is addressing him. What is the name of the God who commands him to return to Egypt and free the Hebrew slaves? Being too modest to demand an answer on his own behalf, Moses puts the question in the mouths of those to whom he will

---

1. In Hebrew, *Ehyeh asher ehyeh*. *Ehyeh* is a first-person singular form of the verb "to be." The tense of the verb indicates an incomplete or open-ended action. Hence, it could mean either "I will be" or "I *continue* to be," depending on the context. For the sake of consistency, and in deference to its later kabbalistic connotation, I translate it as "I will be" throughout.

2. Exod 3:13–14.

The Divine "I-Will-Be"

soon need to explain himself. He asks God what he ought to tell the slaves in Egypt when they ask him who has sent him.

God responds with what appears to be the opposite of an answer: "I will be what I will be." Instead of addressing the question, God rebuffs it. Instead of specifying a name, God rejects the possibility of limiting the identity of the divine.

But in the next breath, God modifies that nonresponse and offers Moses at least a partial answer. God turns what was a statement of divine un-nameability into something like a name: "Thus shall you say to the Israelites: 'I-Will-Be has sent me to you.'" God's refusal to be named has now become God's name—except that, in the process, the two instances of "I will be" in God's original reponse have become a single "I-Will-Be." In transforming an anti-name into a name, God has compressed two statements of divine existence into one.

The talmudic sages wondered what happened to the second instance of the verb "to be" in God's new name. In meeting Moses halfway, why did God abbreviate the original response, dropping half of it?

To answer that question and to teach a lesson of their own, the sages reimagined the dialogue between God and Moses. Reading between the lines, they emended and expanded on the biblical text:

> The blessed Holy One said to Moses, "Go and say to Israel: 'I have been with you during this enslavement, and I will be with you during your [future] enslavements to the empires'" [hence the two instances of the verb "to be"]. Moses answered, "Master of the Universe, it is enough to deal with one trouble at a time!" Therefore the blessed Holy One said, "Go and say to them: 'I-Will-Be has sent me to you'" [hence the single instance of the verb "to be"].[3]

---

3. BT Ber. 9b.

In the course of explaining how two statements of divine being became one, the sages redefined what God and Moses were discussing. They transformed the subject of the conversation from theology to social sensitivity. They took a narrative about divine transcendence, the impossibility of naming the ineffable, and recast it as a story about the proper way to speak to those who are in pain.

They did so by turning the roles of God and Moses upside down. In the original biblical narrative, it is Moses who overreaches by presuming to ask God's name, and it is God who pushes back, putting Moses in his place. In the sages' retelling, however, it is God who overreaches—not by asking a presumptuous question but by promising too much. And it is Moses who pushes back, implicitly rebuking God for doing so.

To be sure, according to the sages, God means well. At first, God declares to Moses, with a double statement of divine being, that just as God is with them in their trials in Egypt, God will be with them in centuries to come, when they will serve under the yoke of the Babylonian, Persian, Greek, and Roman empires. But that is hardly what the people need to hear at this moment. In mentioning the suffering that lies in store for them in the future, God says too much. Magnanimity becomes insensitivity.

Put off by the double declaration, Moses answers: "It is enough to deal with one trouble at a time!" In other words, "Why tell the people about future sufferings when they can hardly bear what they are suffering right now? What need do they have for that extra information?"

God accepts the rebuke and trims back the declaration, saying only what the people need to hear at this moment. God assures Moses—with a single instance of the verb "to be" this time—that God will be with them here and now. That more modest statement of divine being is the name by which God will be known to them from now on.

The Divine "I-Will-Be"

The moral of the story, as the Talmud tells it, is that when we speak to those who are in crisis, we should tailor what we say to their needs, not our own. People who are suffering need reassurance and support where they are now. It is the present that matters, not the distant future. We should say what will be helpful and stop there. Anything beyond that can do more harm than good.

The sages thus replaced a theological message with a practical one. They changed what originally had been a story about divine ineffability, the impossibility of limiting who God is, into a story about tact and empathy. But beneath the surface of their reinterpretation of the biblical text—intentionally or not—the sages gave a hint of what might have been a nascent, unarticulated theology of their own.

Let us consider two implications of the sages' recast narrative. Both flow from their insertion of a single preposition, "with," after the biblical verb "to be." In the original text, the verb "to be"—in both its double and single instances—is absolute. No preposition follows it. No subsequent noun limits it. God says to Moses "I will be what I will be" and comes to a full stop. In the next breath, God adopts the name "I-Will-Be" with no qualifier after it. God's being is unmodified. It is a fact unto itself.

But the sages changed a simple declaration of divine being into a promise of relationship. They transformed the verb "to be"—in both its double and single forms—into "to be *with* . . ." As they retold the story, God assures the people not that God exists in the abstract but that God will be *with them.*

On what basis did the sages insert "with" after the biblical verb "to be"? What gave them license to recast a statement of divine existence into a promise of relationship?

Perhaps the sages were making what they felt to be a reasonable inference based on the previous occurrences of "I will be" in the biblical text. That same form of the verb occurs three times before this in the Hebrew Bible. In each case, it is followed by the words "with you." When Isaac faced a famine, God promised him "I will be *with you*."[4] When Jacob contemplated going home and facing Esau after twenty years of exile, God promised him the same thing: "I will be *with you*."[5] Finally, at the burning bush, just moments before our narrative picks up, God answered Moses's fears about confronting Pharaoh with the same promise: "I will be *with you*."[6]

In each of its three previous occurrences, "I will be" is a promise to be *with*. Perhaps in adding "with" to the fourth occurrence as well, the sages made what they felt to be a reasonable leap based on the textual evidence.

But there is another possibility. Perhaps the sages felt that their revision of the text required no evidence at all, because they did not see it as a leap in the first place. Perhaps they barely noticed themselves adding the word "with" after the verb "to be," because it seemed so obvious to them that it belonged there, that what had been explicit in the first three instances had to be implicit here. Perhaps if we could go back and ask them why they reinterpreted God's being as being *with*, they would respond: "What other way is there to think of it? What could God's existence mean, unless followed by that preposition? A king who has no subjects is no king, after all. If God is God, it can only be in relation to someone else."[7]

Now, let us look at the second implication of the sages' reinterpretation of the biblical story, which also flows from their insertion of the word "with" after "I will be." Even as the added preposition hints at a relational understanding of God's being, it also minimizes God's promised intervention. It prioritizes presence over

---

4. Gen 26:3.
5. Gen 31:3.
6. Exod 3:12.
7. See Pesikta DRK 12:6: "'You are my witnesses, declares the Lord, and I am God' (Isa 43:12). Rabbi Shimon ben Yohai taught: '*If* you are my witnesses, declares the Lord, then I am God. And if you are not my witnesses, it is as if I am not God.'"

The Divine "I-Will-Be"

power. Note that in the biblical text, God pledges much more than merely to be with the Hebrew slaves in their trouble. God promises to rescue them from Egypt and bring them to a land flowing with milk and honey.[8] In the sages' reinterpretation, on the other hand, God's promise to the Hebrew slaves is strangely muted: only to be with them and no more. God makes no pledge to do anything at all, only to be present. Even as the added preposition makes the absolute relational, it also dials back what God offers from intervention to mere accompaniment.

So beneath the surface of the sages' reinterpretation, which seems to eschew theology, we find what may be two implicit pieces of theology after all. Consciously or not, the sages hinted at a God who both exists less independently and is less prone to intervention than the God of the biblical text. The God of the sages' reinterpretation is one whose existence is existence *with* and who offers nothing more than presence.

II

It is hard to know how seriously we should take this as a statement of theology, since it is at best implicit in the talmudic text. What we do know is that centuries later, both claims about the nature of divinity became explicit in the writings of the kabbalists. What the sages hinted at, the kabbalists openly stated. They taught that God's existence is indeed existence with, and that God's power to intervene is fundamentally limited. Moreover, in developing both claims, the kabbalists showed that they are two sides of the same coin.

Let us begin with the first claim, that God exists only in relationship. In the thirteenth century, the authors of the *Zohar*, the classic text of kabbalah, wove that notion into a poetic theological narrative. They taught not only that God needs relationships in

---

8. Exod 3:8.

order to exist as ruler of the world but that God needs relationships in order to exist at all, that God literally has no being except being with. To be sure, the authors of the *Zohar* did not mean that God needs *us* in order to exist. Rather, they believed that the divine came into being through relationships within divinity itself. Not coincidentally, the *Zohar*'s narrative of how that happened is a story about the divine name "I-Will-Be."

That narrative is esoteric and obscure. Let me do my best to summarize it linearly.

Originally, there was only the Infinite.[9] It was everything, and hence nothing. It had no identity, no name, because it had no outer boundaries and no inner distinctions. The Infinite still pervades all that exists. But precisely for that reason, one cannot point to it as something that *is* in itself.

At a certain point, the Infinite, in all its nothingness, began a process of contracting into *somethingness*, of emanating into categories and distinctions. Divinity began to concentrate itself into discrete forms, to become identifiable. The first stage of that process, the first portal in God's journey from the Infinite to the finite, became the first of God's identities, the first of many divine names. That name was "I-Will-Be."[10]

Yet, even though "I-Will-Be" was the first stage of God's process of becoming *something*, the kabbalists still spoke of

---

9. In Hebrew, *Ein Sof*, "the Endless."

10. In the kabbalistic scheme of divine emanations, *Ehyeh* ("I-Will-Be") is also called *Keter* ("Crown"), because it is above the "head" and "body" of divinity, which consist of the remaining emanations.

The Divine "I-Will-Be"

"I-Will-Be" as *nothing*.[11] Or, to say it differently, they understood the name "I-Will-Be" in the sense of "I am not yet."[12]

Why the contradiction? Why did the kabbalists insist that the original divine name was not, in fact, a name? Why did they still call that first stage of divine self-limitation *nothing*? They did so because I-Will-Be still stood alone, above relationship. There was no one yet to call I-Will-Be by name. An identity that cannot be reflected back to its owner is no identity at all.

It was only further down the ladder of divine self-limitation that God came to be identifiable. As subsequent aspects of divinity differentiated themselves, taking on the forms of complementary pairs, the God that we can speak of came into existence through the interplay among those pairs. The divine emanation Wisdom took shape in relation to its partner Insight. The divine emanation Love defined itself in juxtaposition with its counterpart Justice. In other words, in order to be nameable at all, God needed more than one name. God came into existence *with* by virtue of relationships within divinity itself and, ultimately, with the world below.

Thus, the *Zohar* taught explicitly what the sages of the Talmud had taught implicitly. If it is to be intelligible, the divine "I will be" must be followed by the preposition "with." Lacking that

---

11. *Ayin* ("Nothing") is another kabbalistic name for *Keter*/"I-Will-Be." The *Zohar* highlights the nothingness of that first divine emanation in a homily on Gen 1:1, based on the placement of the subject vis-à-vis the verb in the biblical verse. In the Hebrew *B'reishit bara Elohim* ("In the beginning God created"), the subject "God" (*Elohim*) follows the verb "created" (*bara*) instead of preceding it. Taking advantage of that word order, the *Zohar* understands "God" as the *object* of the verb "created" instead of as its subject. In other words, the *Zohar* understands the verse to mean that the knowable "God" was, in a sense, "created" by something else, since the intelligible aspects of divinity emanated out of a deeper source. What, then, is the missing subject of the verb "created"? According to the *Zohar*, it is *Ehyeh* (the divine "I-Will-Be"). The name is missing because it is ineffable (*Zohar* 1:15a; Matt 1:110).

12. Arthur Green speaks of *Ehyeh/Keter* as potential existence, a state of pure open-endedness—hence, "I-Will-Be" as opposed to "I Am" (Green, *Ehyeh*, 5).

qualifier, a statement of divine existence has no meaning. God's being requires otherness.

What of the second implication of that added preposition—namely, that being *with* diminishes God's power? Centuries after the *Zohar*, Rabbi Isaac Luria (1534–72), known as "the Ari," fleshed out that notion.

The Ari pointed out that the self-limitation of which the *Zohar* spoke, the reduction of the Infinite to the finite, is premised on a different kind of self-limitation. The Zoharic contraction *toward*, which made divine relationship and hence divine existence possible, could occur only if it was preceded by contraction *from*. In order to create space for the interactions of distinct and limited aspects of divinity—and all the more so to create space for the world below—the Infinite had to withdraw from that space first. In order for there to be such a thing as otherness, even within divinity itself, there had to be a diminution of divine control.[13]

In other words, what is true for human beings is true for the divine as well. To enter into a relationship, we human beings must contract *toward*. We must compress our thoughts and feelings into words and sentences that will be comprehensible to someone else. But before we can do so, we must first contract *from*. We must step back and make room for the otherness of the person to whom we wish to speak. We must allow that person to be separate from ourselves. The divine, according to the Ari, had to engage in its own version of that two-step process in order to emerge into existence. Before it could emanate into relationships, it had to surrender its omnipotence to make room for the otherness on which relationships depend.

In that way, the Ari taught that the two implications of the sages' added preposition "with" cannot be separated from each other. If God's being is relational, then God's power must be limited. If God's existence is existence *with*, then God's control must

---

13. Scholem, *Major Trends*, 260–61.

The Divine "I-Will-Be"

be attenuated. God's presence with us in our times of trouble, as opposed to active intervention, may be all that we can hope for.

III

We live in a time of skepticism toward theology. For good reasons, we shy away from making detailed and definitive claims about God. As creatures of late modernity, we tend to distrust all grand systems of thought. That is true not only of theologies per se but also of the overarching secular ideologies, the various isms, that modernity itself once substituted for theology. Our vocabulary of meaning tends to be more modest today, and that is a good thing.

But even though I am a creature of this skeptical age—or perhaps because I am—I find that the vision of the *Zohar*, as expanded on by the Ari, helps me to make sense of reality as I encounter it. The only God that I know is a God of presence, not a God of intervention. I have no experience of a God who controls events, but I have known a God whose presence is transformative. The Ari's interpretation of the *Zohar* offers me a way to fit the two sides of my own experience together. It suggests that the positive side—that God is present *with*—cannot be separated from the negative side—that God is no more than present *with*. God's existence in this world requires the mitigation of God's power.

It would be too much, of course, to read all of this back into the Talmud. But it might not be too much to say that the sages, in their reinterpretation of the dialogue between God and Moses, were already moving in that direction. We need not infer a conscious statement of theology on their part, though it is tempting to do so. We need only read the story that they clearly meant to tell, a story about how one ought to speak to people who are struggling. Even at that level, the sages portrayed a God who must say fewer words in order to give comfort, who must take up less space in order to be truly with us. The God of their retelling of the biblical story is a God who learns what all of us must learn: that to be present with others requires restraint, self-limitation. To offer love, one must not promise too much. One must scale down one's words—and oneself—to the needs of the listener. To live in relationship, which is the only way that we can truly live at all, is to live with limits. To be with is to be no more than with.

It might be best for us to stop there. If relationship requires restraint on God's part, that is all the more true for us. If we wish to reciprocate God's presence, to stand before the ineffable, perhaps the less we venture to explain the better. Saying too much, not too little, is the greater risk. Hence, our reticence is for the best. For us, as for the Infinite, the "I will be" of presence is inseparable from the "I will be" of modesty.

The Via Negativa

I

Interpreters of the Ten Commandments have parsed the list in various ways. Since the biblical text itself does not say how the ten are to be numbered—that is, where one commandment ends and the next begins—much depends on where one chooses to divide the paragraphs.

Consider the second commandment. In defining its beginning and its end, the talmudic sages merged what seem to be two prohibitions into one.[1] The commandment, as the sages delineated it, begins:

> You shall have no other gods beside me; you shall not make for yourself a graven image of what is in the heavens above, or on the earth below, or in the waters under the earth. You shall not bow down to them or worship them.[2]

---

1. See, for example, the delineation of the Ten Commandments in Mekh. Bahodesh 8.
2. Exod 20:4–5.

The first clause, "You shall have no other gods," speaks of *whom* we are to worship. At the time of its original composition, it was a call for exclusivity. In referring to "other gods," it acknowledged that such things existed, but it insisted that we leave them to the other nations and serve no god but our own. Later in the biblical period, after monotheism had erased the gods of other nations from the universe of ancient Israel, the clause took on a different meaning. Since the "other gods" that it forbids were now imaginary—no longer competitors but falsehoods—the clause became a call not for exclusivity but for *accuracy*. It became a demand that we serve the true God and reject illusions. In their own time, the talmudic sages understood the passage in that latter sense.[3]

The second clause of the commandment, which begins, "You shall not make for yourself a graven image," speaks of something else. It refers not to whom we worship but to *how*. It commands us to renounce all efforts to depict that which we serve, whether a false god or the true one.[4] It warns us against the temptation to represent divinity, to freeze its form. In that way, it restrains the human tendency toward spiritual arrogance, the impulse to claim mastery of the divine by owning its likeness. It demands that we respect the otherness of that which we revere.[5]

---

3. See, for example, Mekh. Bahodesh 6, which interprets "other gods" to mean (false) gods that "others" worship.

4. Brevard Childs, in his analysis of the Ten Commandments, considers arguments by others that "You shall not make for yourself a graven image" originally prohibited only images of foreign gods. Childs rejects those arguments and concludes that it forbade attempts to represent the God of Israel as well (Childs, *Book of Exodus*, 406–9).

5. Moshe Halbertal and Avishai Margolit suggest that the original reason for the Torah's prohibition of graven images may have been the fear that they impinged on the divine domain—in other words, that they might represent God too well. The authors argue that that explanation better fits the details of the biblical prohibition in that it covered only physical, not verbal, images. Had the Bible's concern been theological error, it ought to have forbidden verbal images as well, as Maimonides ultimately would (Halbertal and Margalit, *Idolatry*, 37–66).

The Via Negativa

It is not clear why the sages chose to merge what seem to be two different prohibitions into one. Why did they conflate all efforts to depict even the true God with the worship of false ones? There was no textual necessity to do so. Centuries earlier, the authors of the Septuagint had made a different choice. They had counted "You shall have no other gods" as the first commandment, and "You shall not make for yourself a graven image" as the second. Given that available alternative, why did the sages choose to treat the worship of false gods and the making of a graven image, even of the true one, as two sides of a single sin?

It is tempting to imagine that the sages linked the two because they understood the second clause as a restatement of the first. If God has no form to depict, then all efforts to portray God must lead us astray. If God transcends all likenesses, then all attempts to represent God must be inaccurate. Though we might mean for them to point to the true God, they must in fact point to "other gods."

But it would be anachronistic to apply that logic to the sages. Most of them freely anthropomorphized the divine. Like their biblical predecessors, they often spoke of God in concrete terms. To be sure, they insisted that God's form is hidden. But to say that it is hidden is to say that it exists. Only something real can be concealed. So it would be hard to argue that the sages thought that *all* graven images must be mistaken.

Why, then, did the sages choose to link all efforts to portray divinity with idol worship, to place the two under a single heading? If they thought that it was possible to capture the form of the true God, at least in theory, why would they equate all attempts to do so with the worship of imaginary gods?

It is hard to say with certainty what their reason was. What we do know is that in merging the two sins, the sages set the stage for their successors, who ultimately would equate the two prohibitions. Centuries later, medieval Jewish philosophers did define all efforts to represent God as inherently mistaken. Since they took it as a given that the true God has no form to portray, they dismissed all attempts to do so as the worship of illusions.

Of all those in that camp, the most emphatic was Moses Maimonides (1135–1204). Following that logic to its radical conclusion, Maimonides prohibited not only physical images of the divine but verbal images as well. He outlawed even sacred metaphors, which reside only in the mind.

Maimonides reasoned in this way: Since God has neither form to represent nor attributes to capture by analogy—in other words, since God is not *like* anything—all likenesses of God must be mistaken. By definition, they portray false gods in that they cannot represent the true one. Hence, the second clause of the commandment flows directly from the first. To serve God and nothing else, we must reject all graven images.

But that logic forced Maimonides to go further. For the same reason, he argued, we must not attempt to capture the divine in words either. We must cleanse our minds of verbal images of God as well. Since God is a singularity to which nothing else can be compared, and since the only way to speak of God at all is to imply a likeness between God and something else, all sacred language, too, must point us toward illusions. Attempts to represent divinity in poetry, no less than in stone, are falsehoods. Far from drawing us toward God, they point us in the opposite direction. To speak of God at all is idol worship.[6]

II

Had Maimonides stopped there—had he rested on the claim that all attempts to represent God, even in our minds, must be idolatrous—he would have left us with a God that is entirely inaccessible, beyond the range of human searching. If we must never speak

---

6. Maimonides, *Guide*, 86 (pt. 1, chap. 59).

of God because all language in which we might try to capture the divine leads us astray, how can there be any spiritual path for us to follow? If we are forbidden to make any effort to conceptualize the object of our journey, how can we take even a first step? Is not such theological purity a spiritual dead end?

Maimonides responded to that question by offering a version of the *via negativa*, the way of negation. He argued that it is not knowing but *un*knowing that provides a path to the divine. Though we can say nothing about who or what God is, we can still deny what God is not, and in that way come closer to the truth. Though we cannot approach God face to face, we can back up, step by step, into the empty space where truth lives due to the exclusion of its opposite. By process of elimination, by discrediting one sacred metaphor after another, we can come to know God by negation. In other words, the renunciation of all sacred images, both physical and mental, can be a journey *toward*, not merely an avoidance of error.

> In the same way as by each additional attribute an object is more specified, and is brought nearer to the true apprehension of the observer, so by each additional negative attribute you advance toward the knowledge of God.... It will now be clear to you that every time you establish by proof the negation of a thing in reference to God, you become more perfect.[7]

In offering negation as a *way*, Maimonides reread the second commandment in another respect. Even as he radically expanded the scope of what its second clause prohibits, he proposed a positive corollary to the commandment as a whole. He reversed the logic of the text and read it as an affirmation—as a *do*, not merely as a *don't*. Not only does the shattering of sacred images, both physical and mental, save us from the worship of false gods, but it brings us closer to the worship of the real one. Not only does

---

7. Maimonides, *Guide*, 84 (pt. 1, chap. 59).

negation guard us against error, but it brings us nearer to the truth. The more illusions we dispel, the more understanding we attain.

In other words, the denial of falsehood is, in itself, a form of revelation. Iconoclasm is not merely a hedge but also a path. In fact, it is the only true path. To be a pilgrim, one must be a skeptic. It is in disbelief, above all, that we meet God.

III

For Maimonides, the via negativa was a journey of the mind. To know God was to purify one's concepts and ideas, to purge the intellect of error. It was to reason one's way into a relationship with the transcendent.

But elsewhere in the Jewish tradition, we find versions of the via negativa that are less cerebral and detached, in which the passions and imagination play a greater role. The kabbalists, who flourished in the centuries after Maimonides, mapped out a version of the via negativa in which the driving force of the religious search is mystical contemplation, not philosophical analysis. Their method was not linear and rational but mythic and symbolic.

At one level, the kabbalists' path to the divine was a reaction against Maimonidean rationalism. In contrast with his austere approach to language, the kabbalists reveled in poetic symbolism. They filled their universe with diverse permutations of divinity, which they invoked with layers upon layers of divine names. They crowded their world with images of the divine, with an array of sacred emanations, all embodying contrasting attributes.

But the paradoxical effect of all those images is to negate each other. By virtue of their sheer abundance, kabbalistic symbols tend to cancel one another out. If God has an endless array of names, God ultimately has no name. If God is everything and its opposite, God in the end is nothing. Arthur Green has argued that although the method of the kabbalists was the antithesis of Maimonidean

The Via Negativa

rationalism, their goal was essentially the same. They, too, sought to attach themselves to the divine through the power of unknowing.[8]

The kabbalists hinted at that method of negation in their definition of idolatry. Idolatry, as they explained it, is the effort to detach a single aspect of divinity from all the others, to treat one sacred metaphor as absolute to the exclusion of its living context. In teaching that God lives only in the push and pull of conflicting images, that no single name can capture God's essence, they guarded against too deep an investment in any one sacred symbol. Implicitly, they undermined the absoluteness of the very images that they relied on in their quest. They taught that journeying toward God requires a certain distance from the images that serve as signposts on the way.

Moreover, the kabbalists taught that at the highest level, God transcends all sacred language. At the endpoint of our journey, all symbols melt away. Behind the layers of divine names, the array of sacred faces, we arrive at *Ayin* ("Nothing"), the original emanation of divinity, closest to the endless unity that underlies all things.[9] For the kabbalists, the ultimate goal of mystical contemplation was to reach the pure white light of nothingness.[10]

Beginning in the eighteenth century, the Hasidic masters offered their own version of the via negativa. On the threshold of modernity, they psychologized the path of which the kabbalists had spoken. They understood the way of negation not as a cosmic journey, an unmasking of the faces of divinity, but as an inner pilgrimage. The idols that they felt the need to shatter were those of the ego and its pretenses, the illusions of control and mastery that our minds inevitably conjure. The negation that they practiced was, above all, the negation of the self.

---

8. See Green, *Judaism for the World*, 5.

9. Other names of that original emanation are *Keter* ("Crown"), *Ehyeh* ("I Will Be"), and *Atika Kadisha* ("Holy Ancient One").

10. Hellner-Eshed, *River Flows from Eden*, 348–51.

The Dancer and the Dance

An early Hasidic master, Yehiel Mikhel of Zloczow (c. 1726–86), taught that version of the via negativa in an interpretation of Deuteronomy 5:5. In that verse, Moses recounts to the Israelites that at Mount Sinai, "I stood between the Lord and you." Yehiel Mikhel understood the "I" of Moses's recounting as a reference to the *I* in general, the ego that obstructs our path to the divine, that stands between God and the human searcher. To know God, we must nullify the self that blocks our view, the very self that hopes to know God in the first place.[11]

In that and a host of similar teachings, the Hasidic masters offered their conception of the via negativa, their Torah of unknowing. To move toward God, they taught, one must strive to make the self transparent, to surrender all presumptions of the ego, to overturn the idol of the *I*.

In the middle of the twentieth century, Abraham Joshua Heschel, an heir to the Hasidic tradition, recast that understanding of the via negativa in a modern form. In an age of technological triumphalism, he taught that the negation of the ego means the humbling of our intellectual arrogance, the deflation of our pretense that we have the power to know all that there is to know. A spiritual journey must begin with the renewal of a "higher incomprehension," with "radical amazement" at the fact that there is anything for science to explain at all:

> What we lack is not a will to believe but a will to wonder .... Awareness of the divine begins with wonder. It is the result of what man does with his higher incomprehension ... The grandeur or mystery of being is not a particular puzzle to the mind, as, for example, the cause of volcanic eruptions. We do not have to go to the end of reasoning to encounter it. Grandeur or mystery is something with which we are confronted everywhere and at all times. Even the very act of thinking baffles our

---

11. Epstein, *Ma'or Vashemesh*, 1:152 (on Parshat Bo). The author, Kalonymus Kalman Epstein (1753–1825), attributes this interpretation of Deut 5:5 to his teacher, Yehiel Mikhel.

thinking, just as every intelligible fact is, by virtue of its being a fact, drunk with baffling aloofness.[12]

For Heschel, as for his Hasidic predecessors, the journey toward God was a journey of self-negation. But he gave that path a new interpretation and invested it with a new urgency. In a world where information often takes the place of wisdom and technological mastery threatens our capacity for awe, Heschel taught that we must start our spiritual journey by deflating a uniquely modern pretense of the ego, the illusion of our intellectual self-sufficiency. We must learn once again to wonder at the mysteries that critical inquiry cannot dispel. Now, more than ever, we must begin our pilgrimage with the renewal of unknowing.

IV

From the Middle Ages to modernity, the via negativa took a range of forms in the Jewish tradition. If we wonder why the notion of negation as a sacred path pervades so many branches of the tradition, the answer may be that it was present in the seed. When we look back to the Hebrew Bible's founding narratives, we recognize a version of the via negativa that was there from the beginning.

From its earliest chapters, the Bible teaches that our path toward God begins with the renunciation of received truths. In Genesis, as God initiates the covenant with Abraham, God calls on him to leave his home, to abandon the civilization that has shaped him, and to set out for an unnamed place which God will show him only when he has arrived there. Unknowing is the very definition of the journey.[13]

---

12. Heschel, *God in Search*, 46–47.
13. Gen 12:1. In Gen. Rabbah 38:13, the sages added an imagined prequel to the story of God's call to Abraham (then Abram). In explaining why God chose him, they taught that Abram, the son of an idol maker, had literally shattered his father's gods.

In Exodus, the God who calls to Moses from the burning bush is an elusive God, whose name is nothing but a form of namelessness: "I will be what I will be."[14] To follow this God, Moses and the Hebrew slaves—like Abraham before them—will have to leave behind all that they know and venture out into an empty wilderness. Only there, in a place devoid of false gods, will they be able respond to the true one. Only on a path without landmarks will they be able to find their way. Their forty years of wandering will be a journey of negation, a struggle to unlearn the truths that made them slaves, to find the freedom to embrace a mystery.

This older version of the via negativa, embedded in the Bible's narrative, is neither philosophical like that of Maimonides, nor mystical like that of the kabbalists and the Hasidic masters. We might call it practical. It does not begin with rigorous claims about the unknowability of God, or with a yearning to transcend our ego or the limits of our understanding. It begins with a more pragmatic insight. Its message is that if we wish to find a God that the prevailing culture does not know, we must be prepared to break with the assumptions of that culture. If we seek a God who stands outside existing pantheons, we must free ourselves from what we have been trained to think and venture into emptiness. Discontinuity is a prerequisite for spiritual renewal.

The sages crystallized that older, more pragmatic understanding of the via negativa in a comment on the meaning of the desert in the Bible's narrative of revelation.

> "God spoke to Moses in the desert of Sinai" (Num 1:1). One who does not make oneself like an ownerless desert cannot receive wisdom and Torah. Hence it says "in the desert of Sinai."[15]

Only in a state of being unowned, like the desert, can we answer the call of a hidden God. Only when we break free of the

---

14. Exod 3:14.
15. Num. Rabbah 1:7.

gravity of unexamined cultural axioms can we feel the pull of a more distant star.

This teaching hints at an answer to our original question: Why did the sages define the second commandment as they did? If, unlike their medieval successors, they thought that it was theoretically possible to depict the form of the true God, why did they equate attempts to do so with the worship of *false* gods?

Perhaps they did not mean for us to take that linkage as a strict equation, in the way that later teachers would. Perhaps their goal in linking the two prohibitions was to make a more practical point, to teach this older version of the via negativa. In other words, perhaps they meant to recapitulate the narrative in which the Ten Commandments are embedded, to echo a core message of the story of our journey to Mount Sinai. That message is that if we wish to serve the God who brought us out of Egypt, we must question everything that we thought we knew. Conventional assumptions, truths carved in stone, are unlikely to bring us closer to the God of liberation. If we wish to walk with that God, iconoclasm is the most reliable path.

If that was the sages' intent, their point applies more urgently than ever in our time. In an age that tends to polarize us into opposing camps, searchers and skeptics—those who urgently seek meaning and those who have no patience for illusions—the sages' message serves as a corrective. It reminds us that authentic skepticism, far from undermining our spiritual quest, is a prerequisite to it. To be a pilgrim, one must deepen one's capacity to doubt.

Today, skepticism toward received truths is a powerful cultural current, and that is something to be grateful for. But like all such currents, it can easily freeze into an orthodoxy of its own. Having shattered old creeds, the skeptical intellect is tempted to substitute new ones. In particular, it suffers from the tendency to shrink reality to fit its own dimensions, and, in the process, to deplete the power of language. In that sense, the liberation of the modern mind can turn into a prison of its own.

How do we escape that Egypt? Not by suppressing doubt but by intensifying it, not by being less skeptical but by being more so. To seek God in a time of spiritual constriction, now as in the past, we must detach ourselves from unexamined assumptions. To be sure, no one can rise entirely above the limits of one's time and place. But one can criticize those limits from within. That is the task of every generation, including our own.

The lesson of the via negativa, in its original form, is that we discover the divine not by acquiescing to conventional answers but by deepening our questions, not by submitting to accepted truths but by freeing ourselves from them. If we are to meet God, it will be in the place where we always have: in mystery. In the desert, now as in the past, we find our way.

Bibliography

Arendt, Hannah. *The Origins of Totalitarianism*. New York: Harcourt, 1968.
Arnold, Matthew. "Dover Beach." In *The Norton Anthology of Poetry*, edited by Alexander W. Allison et al., 850–51. New York: W. W. Norton & Company, 1975.
Borowitz, Eugene. *Renewing the Covenant: A Theology for the Post-Modern Jew*. Philadelphia: Jewish Publication Society, 1991.
Buber, Martin. "The Silent Question." In *On Judaism: Martin Buber*, edited by Nahum Glatzer, 202–13. New York: Schocken, 1967.
Childs, Brevard S. *The Book of Exodus: A Critical, Theological Commentary*. Louisville: Westminster, 1974.
Descartes, René. *Meditations on the First Philosophy*. In *The Rationalists*, 97–175. Translated by John Veitch. New York: Anchor, 1974.
Einstein, Albert. "Religion and Science." *New York Times*, November 9, 1930. https://timesmachine.nytimes.com/timesmachine/1930/11/09/92114511.html?pageNumber=136.
Epstein, Kalonymus Kalman. *Ma'or Vashemesh*. Jerusalem: Gallim, 1986.
Fish, Stanley. *The Trouble with Principle*. Cambridge: Harvard University Press, 1999.
Fowler, James. *Stages of Faith: The Psychology of Human Development and the Quest for Meaning*. New York: Harper & Row, 1981.
Gillman, Neil. *Sacred Fragments: Recovering Theology for the Modern Jew*. Philadelphia: Jewish Publication Society, 1990.
Goff, Philip. *Galileo's Error: Foundations for a New Science of Consciousness*. New York: Pantheon, 2019.
Gould, Stephen Jay. "Non-Overlapping Magisteria." *Natural History* 106 (March 1997) 16–22. http://www.blc.arizona.edu/courses/schaffer/449/Gould%20Nonoverlapping%20Magisteria.htm.
Green, Arthur. *Ehyeh: A Kabbalah For Tomorrow*. Woodstock, VT: Jewish Lights, 2003.
———. *Judaism for the World: Reflections on God, Life, and Love*. New Haven, CT: Yale University Press, 2020.

BIBLIOGRAPHY

———. *Radical Judaism: Rethinking God & Tradition.* New Haven, CT: Yale University Press, 2010.
Halbertal, Moshe, and Avishai Margalit. *Idolatry.* Cambridge: Harvard University Press, 1992.
Hellner-Eshed, Melila. *A River Flows from Eden: The Language of Mystical Experience in the Zohar.* Stanford, CT: Stanford University Press, 2009.
Heschel, Abraham Joshua. *God in Search of Man.* New York: Farrar, Straus & Giroux, 1955.
Jacobs, Louis. *A Jewish Theology.* London: Darton, Longman & Todd, 1973.
James, William. "The Will to Believe." In *Essays on Faith and Morals: William James,* edited by Ralph Barton Perry, 32–62. Cleveland: Meridian, 1962.
Maimonides, Moses. *Guide for the Perplexed.* Translated by M. Friedlander. New York: Dover, 1956.
Marvell, Andrew. "To His Coy Mistress." In *The Norton Anthology of Poetry,* edited by Alexander W. Allison et al., 370–71. New York: W. W. Norton & Company, 1975.
Matt, Daniel C. *God and the Big Bang: Discovering Harmony between Science and Spirituality.* Woodstock, VT: Jewish Lights, 1996.
———. *The Zohar.* Pritzker ed. Vols. 1, 4. Stanford, CA: Stanford University Press, 2004, 2007.
Nagel, Thomas. *Mind and Cosmos: Why the Materialist Neo-Darwinian Conception of Nature is Almost Certainly False.* Oxford: Oxford University Press, 2012.
———. *The View from Nowhere.* Oxford: Oxford University Press, 1986.
Petuchowski, Jakob. *Ever Since Sinai: A Modern View of Torah.* Milwaukee, WI: B. Arbit, 1979.
Ricoeur, Paul. *The Symbolism of Evil.* Boston: Beacon, 1969.
Rosenzweig, Franz. "On Jewish Learning: From the Draft of the Address at the Opening of the Freis Judisches Lehrhaus in Frankfurt." In *Franz Rosenzweig: His Life and Thought,* edited by Nahum Glatzer, 228–34. New York: Schocken, 1953.
Scholem, Gershom G. *Major Trends in Jewish Mysticism.* New York: Schocken, 1941.
Schwarz, Sidney. "It Is Called Covenantal Community." *JewishInsider,* November 28, 2017. https://ejewishphilanthropy.com/it-is-called-covenantal-community/.
Tillich, Paul. *Dynamics of Faith.* New York: Harper & Row, 1957.
Yeats, William Butler. "Among School Children." In *The Collected Poems of W. B. Yeats,* 212–14. New York: Macmillan, 1951.

www.ingramcontent.com/pod-product-compliance
Lightning Source LLC
Chambersburg PA
CBHW070932160426
43193CB00011B/1667